HAUNTED WASHINGTON, DC

Federal Phantoms, Government Ghosts,
and Beltway Banshees

Tom Ogden

Globe
Pequot

Guilford, Connecticut

Globe Pequot

An imprint of Rowman & Littlefield

Distributed by NATIONAL BOOK NETWORK

Copyright © 2016 by Tom Ogden

British Library Cataloguing in Publication Information available

Library of Congress Cataloging-in-Publication Data

Names: Ogden, Tom, author.
Title: Haunted Washington, DC : federal phantoms, government ghosts, and beltway banshees / Retold by Tom Ogden.
Description: Guilford, Connecticut : Globe Pequot, 2016.
Identifiers: LCCN 2016007099 (print) | LCCN 2016008230 (ebook) | ISBN 9781493019403 (pbk. : alk. paper) | ISBN 9781493019410 (ebook)
Subjects: LCSH: Haunted places—Washington (D.C.) | Ghosts—Washington (D.C.)
Classification: LCC BF1472.U6 O45 2016 (print) | LCC BF1472.U6 (ebook) | DDC 133.109753—dc23

For Patrick A. Kelley

CONTENTS

CONTENTS

CONTENTS

ACKNOWLEDGMENTS

It would have been impossible for me to complete *Haunted Washington, DC* without the help and support of many people. As always, my thanks go out to Mark Willoughby, Joan Lawton, Michael Kurland and Linda Robertson, Dustin Stinett, and David Shine for their feedback and suggestions.

Thanks, too, to my editor Amy Lyons, original project editor Tracee Williams, assistant production editor Caroline McManus, copy editor Michelle Peters, and proofreader Roberta Monaco for their guidance and extreme patience. Also thanks to Erin Turner for her continued assistance.

INTRODUCTION

Those of you who have read any of my other books in the *Haunted* series—and if you have, I thank you—you know that my take on ghost stories is somewhat different than that of other authors.

I love the thrills and chills of a good horror story—the Boo Factor. But for a tale to stand the test of time, I think it has to be more than just myth and make-believe. There has to be at least a kernel of truth for a claim to stick around for a century or more.

Historical ghost stories that involve actual people, periods, and places from the past are my favorites, and they're a special subset in paranormal literature. As I retell these popular legends, I try to be a paranormal journalist.

What do I mean by that? Well, it's all well and good to crawl through a cemetery with a thermometer in one hand, an EMF meter in the other, and an infrared GoPro strapped to your head. (In fact, it can be quite fun.)

But over time, ghost legends often become convoluted, sometimes with a dozen or more variations. First, I compare and contrast the many versions of a story for discrepancies. I continue to dig until I unearth as many details as I can about the alleged haunting. In the end, I try to "report" my findings in a way that's informative as well as entertaining. In this particular book, I hope to give you a real feel for the Washington in which our ghosts live.

Modern-day Washington, DC, is fairly compact—only 68.3 square miles—but negotiating it can be quite daunting to the novice. As a result, I've divided the book into five parts, each one dedicated to a portion of the city's haunted sites.

I start at the White House, one of the country's most recognizable landmarks. There are so many ghost stories associated with this one building that I've reserved the entire section for the Executive Mansion. I've placed all of its spooky legends into a single chapter.

Part Two investigates Capitol Hill, home to the buildings that house the nation's legislative and judicial branches as well as many other noteworthy paranormal hot spots.

Part Three takes us to Lafayette Square, which is across the street from the north lawn of the White House. Amazingly, there are almost a half dozen sites within that single square block harboring apparitions, all dating to the nineteenth century.

Part Four hops over to Georgetown. Nestled in the northwest corner of the city, Georgetown predates Washington, DC, but it was incorporated into the District when the capital was founded in 1790. Several of Georgetown's houses, bridges, and riverbanks are rife with wraiths.

Part Five contains a hodgepodge or potpourri of other haunted structures scattered throughout the rest of the District of Columbia.

Three appendices follow. As with all of my books in this series, Appendix A is a selective bibliography of the books and websites I consulted during my research. Appendix B contains the contact information for all of the organized ghost tours that operate in and around Washington. This includes several walking tours of Old Town Alexandria on the west side of the Potomac. Appendix C lists the names and addresses (and, when possible, telephone numbers and websites) for all of the haunted sites mentioned in *Haunted Washington, DC*.

This book is being released in a presidential election year, so all eyes are turned to the nation's capital. What a perfect time to examine the city's hidden history along with its many ghosts and spirits.

PROLOGUE

Before we jump into our ghost stories of Washington, DC—and don't worry, there are plenty of them—I thought we should take a moment to reflect on why and how the district was formed. If you're a scholar of the American Revolution, feel free to skip the first few paragraphs.

Spoiler alert: There was a war, and the Americans won.

Okay, as you all remember from your history lessons in elementary school, by 1770 the British settlements along the eastern coast of North America had been divided into thirteen separate colonies. Each had autonomous rule but, in the end, they all answered to the British crown. A series of major disputes with Parliament—the most infamous objection being "taxation without representation"—led to representatives from all of the colonies except Georgia getting together in Philadelphia in the fall of 1774. Their goal was to craft a list of grievances to send to King George III back in London. The petition from this First Continental Congress fell on deaf ears.

The seriousness of the situation came to a head on April 19, 1775, with the Battles of Lexington and Concord. The Continental Congress reconvened in Philadelphia with many of the same delegates on May 10, 1775, to discuss their options. (Noteworthy among new arrivals were John Hancock, Benjamin Franklin, and, eventually, a delegation from Georgia.) Then on June 17, 1775, came the Battle of Bunker Hill. For all intents and purposes, the American Revolution had begun, but it took another full year of deliberation until the Second Continental Congress finally declared independence on July 4, 1776.

Over the course of the ensuing war, the Continental Congress was forced to move for a time to Baltimore, then later to Lancaster and York in Pennsylvania. In all, Congress would meet in eight different "capitals" before the formation of Washington, DC. Delegates enacted the Articles of the Confederation, which defined a limited role for the national government. It took until March 1, 1781, for the states to ratify the document, by which time Congress was back in Philadelphia. It would be another seven months until the war came to a close on October 19, 1781, with the Battle of Yorktown. The Treaty of Paris officially ended the war on September 3, 1783.

With the conflict over, the colonies recognized that there was a need to modify its loose Articles of Confederation, so they sent representatives back to Philadelphia in May 1787. The delegates immediately elected George Washington their president. It soon became apparent that a revision of the Articles was not enough. A stronger document was needed for the new country. After heated debate, the Constitutional Convention (as the gathering became known) adopted and signed the United States Constitution on September 17, 1787.

That December, Delaware became the first state to adopt the Constitution. It became the law of the land on June 21, 1788, after the ninth state ratified it. Rhode Island became the last of the original colonies to ratify the document in May 1790.

Meanwhile, in September 1788, the final Congress under the Articles of Confederation met one last time to set up national elections for the new Congress, the president, and vice president. On April 6, 1789, the Electoral College unanimously named George Washington the first president of the United States, and the Father of Our Country was inaugurated twenty-four days later.

Okay, so how did Washington, DC, come about?

In 1783 a throng of Revolutionary soldiers had converged on Congress to demand their back pay from the War of Independence. Fearing for their safety, delegates asked the Pennsylvania governor to call up the state militia to protect them, but the governor refused. That indignity was high on the representatives' minds when, meeting back in Philadelphia in 1787 to write the US Constitution, they gave the federal government the power to create a national capital where they could control all of the laws and not worry about interference from (or depend upon) any of the states.

Obviously, the land would have to be ceded by one or more states or purchased by Congress, and it was decided that the new federal district could not exceed "ten miles square," or 100 square miles. Once the property was acquired, the legislature would have total authority over it and any "Forts, Magazines, Arsenals, dock-Yards and other needful Buildings" that were erected. The ruling didn't stipulate where the "Seat of Government" had to be located.

Four states offered territory, but after much negotiation Congress accepted land from just Maryland and Virginia as part of the 1790 Residence Act. According to the law, the new district had to be somewhere on the Potomac River between the mouths of the Conococheague Creek and the Anacostia River, then known as the Eastern Branch. In addition to the land given up by the states, nineteen private landowners had to be convinced to relinquish their property.

The Resolution Act allowed the President (who, of course, was George Washington) to select the actual location within those boundaries. Washington wanted to include Alexandria, Virginia, in the capital, but some legislators were concerned that its inclusion might be perceived as a conflict of interest: Washington's personal estate, Mount Vernon, was only seven miles downriver from Alexandria. A 1791 compromise barred any federal buildings from being erected on the Virginia side of the Potomac. Thus, even though a third of the *district* would extend onto the south or west bank of the river, the entire *city* of Washington had to be located north and east of the Potomac. When all was said and done, the new capital was officially named the Territory of Columbia and its primary town was dubbed the City of Washington, or as we know it today, Washington, DC.

Surveyors laid out the city as a square or diamond shape. Its corners were located at the four points of the compass, with Jones Point as its southernmost position. With ten straight miles between each of the cardinal points, the district contains exactly one hundred square miles, the maximum allowable acreage.

President Washington originally tapped civil engineer Pierre Charles L'Enfant to design the layout of the city. The architect's plan fanned out from a Capitol building that would be erected on Jenkins Hill, now called Capitol Hill. Numbered roads would follow a north-south and east-west grid pattern, along with several grand avenues (now named for states) cutting on a diagonal. An especially wide thoroughfare would run along the district's east-west axis for about a mile between the Capitol and the Potomac. That avenue was never constructed, but its pathway is now the

National Mall. There would also be a number of canals crossing the district.

(Contrary to popular belief, the Capitol Building was not located at the geographic center of the District. But by drawing imaginary lines between the north-south and east-west axes with the Capitol at its center, the district is neatly divided into four very unequal administrative quadrants: Northeast, Northwest, Southeast, and Southwest. In later years, the initials NE, NW, SE, and SW would be affixed to street addresses to indicate the quadrant in which buildings are located.)

L'Enfant delivered his plan to Washington in 1791, but over the next year the architect battled with three city commissioners over the design, eventually leading to the president having to dismiss L'Enfant. One of those commissioners, Andrew Ellicott, made several changes to L'Enfant's drawings, and it's his revised map that became the blueprint for the city.

Construction on the new town began shortly thereafter, and in 1800 Congress moved to Washington, DC, from Philadelphia. Work on the city's buildings and infrastructure had a brief but major setback on August 24, 1814, when British troops under the command of Major General Robert Ross invaded during the War of 1812. Government officials, including President James Madison, had to flee as many of the federal buildings were set ablaze.

That evening, a tremendous thunderstorm put out most of the flames, but a subsequent tornado did further damage. Ross withdrew his men back to their ships, and the British moved on, leaving much of Washington decimated. In all, they had occupied the city for about twenty-six hours.

The White House and Capitol Building were empty shells. There was a short-lived but intense discussion over whether the capital should be relocated, but Congress voted to stay in Washington. Representatives and senators met in the hastily constructed Old Brick Capitol building until restoration of the original Capitol was completed in 1819. For the remainder of Madison's term, a private home known as the Octagon House served as the Executive Residence. James Monroe was able to move into a partially restored Presidential Mansion upon his inauguration in 1817.

Railroads linked DC to the rest of the country beginning in 1831. Residents of Alexandria, increasingly upset that federal construction was limited to the other side of the Potomac by law, petitioned Congress and Virginia to return (or retrocede) their part of the District of Columbia to the state. Surprisingly, both parties agreed to the request, and in 1847 the thirty-nine square miles south of the Potomac once again became part of Virginia. That area included what is today Alexandria and Arlington County.

Up until the Civil War, many of DC's residents left the city during the summer when Congress was not in session. The government had to remain in Washington during the War Between the States, however, so defensive forts were built for protection. As it turned out, there was only one attack on the capital during the entire conflict. The city's population swelled after the war, forcing necessary improvements in roads and sanitation. In the 1870s the ostensibly independent city of Georgetown was completely merged into Washington when the last independent school, police, and other civic councils came under the complete control of a Congressional Board of Commissioners. In the 1880s, the last of the city canals was filled in, and in 1884 the Washington Monument was completed. Then in 1900, Congress formed the McMillan Commission to oversee the city's redevelopment and the creation of the National Mall.

So let's jump ahead a century.

Today, Washington, DC, houses the three branches of federal government, all of its major agencies, and close to two hundred foreign embassies. Thousands of government employees flood into town each day, and millions of tourists visit annually. More than 650,000 people call the city home.

Of primary importance to readers, the capital's two centuries of history have led to hundreds of ghosts, phantoms, spirits, apparitions, spectres, and banshees—call them what you will—taking up residence within its "ten miles square."

Let's meet a few.

Part One

THE WHITE HOUSE

When the American colonies threw off the binds of Great Britain, most of the new country's citizens agreed they didn't want to be ruled by another monarch. The federal government should be a representative democracy with an elected head of state. As a result, the president wouldn't be given a palace for his residence, but he still needed a place to live.

Each administration has gracefully turned over the keys to the White House to its next occupant. But some of the presidents have returned as spirits long after their time in office was complete. And a few of the First Ladies have shown up as well.

Chapter 1

Executive Mansion Mysteries

THE WHITE HOUSE
1600 PENNSYLVANIA AVENUE NW

Have you ever lived in a place that you loved so much you hoped you would never have to leave? Well, apparently some of America's chief executives, first ladies, guests, and staff have felt the same way about the White House.

The White House is one of the most familiar landmarks in the country, if not the world. The three-story structure acts as the residence for the nation's commander in chief.

So let's get right to the point: The White House is said to be one of the most haunted buildings in Washington, DC. And it's had that reputation almost from the start. Before we dive into all the folklore, it makes sense to take a look at the building's history, including the layout of the rooms and how their purposes have changed over the decades. The mansion's storied past will help us visualize where the ghostly manifestations occur—and why.

At the time of George Washington's presidential inauguration, his personal home was his Virginia plantation, Mount Vernon. Congress was still meeting in New York City, so from April 1789 to August 1790 it rented two private mansions to act as his residence, first, the Samuel Osgood House, then later the Alexander Macomb House. The State of New York started construction on Government House, which would have become the official executive residence, but before it could be completed, the federal government moved to Philadelphia. A house was secured there for Washington, and he lived in it for the rest of his presidency. President John Adams stayed in the same house until May 1800.

It was a given that a presidential palace would be constructed in the federal district established by the 1790 Residence Act. The mansion's location was prominently featured on Pierre Charles L'Enfant's original plan for the city, but it was decided a competition would be held for the building's design. Washington, meeting with several city commissioners, selected the one submitted by architect James Hoban. (Washington's choice may have been influenced by his having previously seen Hoban's Charleston County Courthouse in South Carolina.)

Hoban's blueprints for the Executive Mansion no longer exist, but it's known that Washington asked for changes to the original Neoclassical design, resulting in the eleven-bay-window façade seen today.

Construction on the residence began on October 13, 1792, and from the beginning the place was known by many different names, including the President's House, the President's Mansion, the President's Palace, the Presidential Mansion, and the Executive Mansion. Legend suggests that the building acquired the nickname "the White House" because it was painted white to hide scorch marks after it was burned by the British in 1814, but there are printed references to the "White House" as early as 1811. More likely the building got the name because the sandstone mansion was covered with a layer of limestone, which was then painted white. President Theodore Roosevelt officially used the term "White House" in 1901.

The first president to take up occupancy was John Adams, who moved into the partially completed structure on November 1, 1800. His residency was short-lived, because President Thomas Jefferson took office on March 4, 1801. Jefferson made the first major alteration to the house, adding a terrace lined with columns to each side of the building. Now known as the East and West Colonnades, the extensions were decorative and hid the stables, laundry, and other outbuildings.

Because the White House was gutted during the Burning of Washington, President James Madison was invited to use the (now haunted) Octagon House as his presidential home. He stayed for a year and then moved into one of the group of houses known as the Seven Buildings for the rest of his term. The White House was rebuilt by the time James Monroe was inaugurated in 1817.

Until 1900, the president's executive business was usually conducted on the second floor of the White House, but it was always apparent more office space was needed. In 1902, Theodore Roosevelt had a West Wing constructed and moved his personal office (the Oval Office), the cabinet room, and all of the support staff there. It was a separate two-story building located, as its name suggests, to the west of the Executive Residence, with its first floor on the same level as the ground floor of the White House. The two structures are connected by Jefferson's West Colonnade. The building has been renovated and reconfigured many times, most notably by President Franklin D. Roosevelt, who moved the Oval Office to its southeast corner. The new (and current) location allowed easier and discrete access for

FDR's wheelchair, and it had the added benefit of overlooking the Rose Garden.

Theodore Roosevelt had added a small building to the east of the White House as an entranceway for formal and public gatherings. During the Truman Administration, it was expanded into the two-story East Wing, connected to the White House by the East Colonnade. It has acted as the Office of the First Lady since Rosalynn Carter moved her office and staff there in 1977. Visitors to the White House often enter through the East Wing.

So now let's move on to the Executive Residence itself.

When seen from the north, the ground level of the building is hidden behind what was once a raised carriage ramp. The front portico was added around 1830. At the center of the southern façade, the mansion has a semicircular protrusion to accommodate the inclusion of oval-shaped rooms in the floor plans. (These rooms are not to be confused with the present-day Oval Office. Oval rooms were a fashionable architecture feature in the late eighteenth century.) Around 1824, James Monroe added the large, curved portico on the south side of the building that overlooks the White House lawn.

For the building's first hundred years or so, the ground floor acted as a cellar. Today it holds the kitchen; the library; the offices for the curator, housekeeper, and doctor; the map room; two meeting rooms; and, in the oval space at the center of the south side, the Diplomatic Reception Room. Two additional basement levels have since been added beneath the ground floor.

The first floor of the White House is often referred to as the State Floor (or Floor of State), because this is where formal receptions and dinners are held. Guests to special events such as these would come through the North Portico into a grand entrance hall. Directly across a long hallway are the oval Blue Room, flanked by the Green Room and the Red Room. To the far left is the large East Room, used for soirees and entertainment; to the far right is the State Dining Room. (The family's private dining room is also on this level.)

The second floor is the First Family's primary residence. It contains the bedrooms, sitting rooms, and guest rooms, including the East and West Bedrooms, the Queens' Bedroom, and the Lincoln Bedroom. The Yellow Oval Room at the middle of the south façade opens onto the Truman Balcony.

The third floor was originally an attic. Prior to a renovation in 1902, it was used mostly for storage. It also had eight small bedrooms for servants. The space was expanded under subsequent presidents until it was almost as large as the floors below it. Because it sits back from the parapet, the third floor is mostly hidden when the building is viewed from ground level. In additional to several modest bedrooms and some storage, the third floor contains offices, a small gymnasium, a solarium, and other spaces for relaxation.

Now let's go on a ghost hunt.

The White House has had a reputation for being haunted since the mid-nineteenth century. Its many apparitions have been seen by presidents, their families, staff, guests, and visitors alike, and they pop in to this day.

President Truman, for example, was very aware of the White House revenants. In June 1945, two months after assuming the presidency, he wrote his wife Bess:

> I sit here in this old house and work on foreign
> affairs, read reports, and work on speeches—all the

while listening to the ghosts walk up and down the hallway and even right in here in the study. . . . At 4 o'clock I was awakened by three distinct knocks on my bedroom door. No one was there. Damn place is haunted, sure as shootin'. . . . The floors pop and the drapes move back and forth—I can just imagine old Andy and Teddy having an argument over Franklin.

Our search for paranormal mischief in the White House starts on the first floor. The ghost of Anna Surratt allegedly appears outside on the North Portico annually on the night of July 6th. The spectre silently screams and bangs her fists against the White House doors, trying to gain entrance to beg for the life of her mother to be spared—just like she did in real life in 1865. Anna was the daughter of Mary Surratt, the condemned coconspirator who owned the boarding house where the Lincoln assassins plotted their crime. Anna's pleas were ignored, and, on the morning of July 7th, Mary Surratt became the first woman to be hanged for a federal crime. Now, every year, on the anniversary of Anna's attempt to gain entry to the White House, her spirit returns to repeat her eternal, unsuccessful entreaty. There are also reports that she sometimes materializes on July 7th as well, sitting on the portico steps.

In addition to Anna Surratt, the spectre of a British soldier carrying a torch and wearing an early nineteenth-century uniform has been spotted on the North Portico. He's thought to be one of the infantrymen who set fire to the building during the War of 1812. Also on the North Portico and entranceway, several former doormen and White House ushers, all long dead, sometimes return to their posts, welcoming startled guests.

Inside on the first floor, the apparition of one of the mansion's earliest occupants materializes in the East Room. It's Abigail Adams, wife of the second president. It's said that Abigail would often hang her laundry in the East Room to dry. Today her apparition, dressed in a mobcap, apron, and shawl, is seen entering, exiting, and inside the East Room. Her arms are stretched out in front of her as if she were holding a large basket of laundry. Her ghost was frequently seen during the Taft Administration, but members of a tour group claimed to have seen Adams as recently as 2002. Some people have also reported the strong scent of laundry detergent in the room.

Down the hall from the East Room, the Blue Oval Room plays host to the spirit of President John Tyler. Also seen there is Frances Folsom Cleveland, who married President Grover Cleveland in the room in 1886. Her phantom returned to the chamber soon after her death in 1947.

Up on the second floor, a disembodied voice has been heard in the Yellow Oval Room. Cesar Carrera, Franklin D. Roosevelt's valet, first reported it after the phantom called him by name. The spirit identified himself as David Burns, the man who sold the federal government much of the land that makes up the City of Washington, including the ground on which the White House sits. Burns isn't heard often these days; the last known report was from a security guard during the Truman administration. (Some sources say the guard, who was standing in the Yellow Oval Room at the time, heard the sound coming from the attic overhead.)

The faint strains of violin music have been heard in the Yellow Oval Room. The musician is President Thomas Jefferson, known for his exceptional ability on the instrument. He's returned from the Beyond to serenade visitors.

He usually remains invisible, but Mary Todd Lincoln saw his ghost in the room. She ran into the phantom of President John Tyler there as well.

Not to be outdone, the British soldier from the North Portico also frequents the Yellow Oval Room and the adjacent hallway.

The loud laughter, cursing, and stomping of President Andrew Jackson's ghost has been heard throughout the mansion and was first reported by Mary Todd Lincoln. But the spirit has most often been associated with the Queens' Bedroom on the second floor. Before 1902 the suite usually acted as the bedroom and office for the president's private secretary. When the presidential staff moved to the West Wing, the chamber was refurbished and renamed the Rose Room. It was rechristened the Queens' Bedroom in 1963 to honor the female European heads of state that have stayed there.

(Visiting dignitaries and foreign rulers have been overnight guests in the White House in the past, but they now usually choose to reside at Blair House, the president's official guesthouse located on the other side of Pennsylvania Avenue.)

Why would the phantom of Andrew Jackson return to the Queens' Bedroom in particular? Well, tradition has it the bed most frequently used to furnish it once belonged to Old Hickory himself. (It was donated to the Executive Mansion in 1902.) The seventh president may also have used the suite as his bedroom. One of President Lyndon Johnson's aides heard Jackson swearing in the Queens' Bedroom in 1964, and in her 1961 autobiography *My Thirty Years Backstairs at the White House*, seamstress Lillian Rogers Parks said that while doing some sewing in the room she sensed

Jackson's presence. She felt an invisible hand grasp the back of her chair as the unseen person, whom she believed to be Jackson, leaned over her. Parks also noticed the room had become quite cold. Others have felt a cold spot on the bed itself. (A cold spot—a focused, often-cylindrical shaft of icy air—is thought by many paranormalists to be evidence of a spirit or perhaps a portal between this world and the next.) A few sources say that staff members have seen Jackson's spectre, but in most versions of the legend his ghost never appears.

The most famous spirit materialization connected with the Queens' Bedroom wasn't by Andrew Jackson. It was by the building's most famous resident apparition, Abraham Lincoln. Honest Abe's ghost was an almost-frequent guest during FDR's twelve years in the White House, from 1933 to 1945. Queen Wilhelmina of the Netherlands visited during that period, and a popular legend says she encountered Lincoln's spectre while staying in what was then the Rose Room. Late one evening she was awakened by a knock at her door. Opening it, she was shocked to see Lincoln's very recognizable visage, complete with frock coat and stovepipe top hat, standing in the hallway in front of her. Like any proud lady of her station, she immediately fainted. The next day she told guests at a reception about her other-worldly visitor. (Another telling of the tale says the queen saw the spirit but didn't recognize him. When Eleanor Roosevelt explained the next morning that Wilhelmina had seen Lincoln's ghost, the monarch politely said her goodbyes and hurriedly left the city.)

Lincoln's ghost haunts the White House more than any other apparition and has been seen in the greatest number of places, including the chamber that's immediately across the corridor from the Queens' Bedroom: the Lincoln Bedroom. (Indeed, some sources say that Queen Wilhelmina was staying in the Lincoln Bedroom, not the Rose Room, when she saw the Great Emancipator's ghost.) Interestingly, the so-called Lincoln Bedroom was not where Lincoln slept. Instead, he used the space as an office and a meeting room for his Cabinet. When the executive offices moved to the West Wing in 1902, the second-story bedchamber, with sitting room, and bath were converted into the Blue Suite. Herbert Hoover later made it his private office. His wife, Lou, added Civil War–era furnishings, and the room became known as the Lincoln Study. It once again functioned as a bedroom suite under President Franklin D. Roosevelt, but it wasn't until President Truman placed the "Lincoln bed" there that it was called the Lincoln Bedroom. (There's some question as to whether President Lincoln ever slept in the bed or whether it simply dates to his time in office.)

During one visit, Sir Winston Churchill occupied the suite. After taking an evening bath, the prime minister walked into the adjoining bedroom completely naked (except for the ever-present cigar in his mouth). He was surprised to see the silent spirit of Abraham Lincoln, standing by the fireplace leaning on the mantel. Churchill, ever ready with a quip, blustered, "Good evening, Mr. President. You seem to have me at a disadvantage." Lincoln smiled wryly, then vanished. For the rest of his stay, and during subsequent sojourns, the British Bulldog occupied the Rose Room.

Over the years, several White House staffers have seen the sixteenth president's spectre lying on the bed in the Lincoln Bedroom. Others have spotted him sitting on the edge of the bed, removing or pulling on his boots. These witnesses include Eleanor Roosevelt's secretary, Mary Eben, who screamed and ran out of the room. President Reagan's daughter Maureen poked fun at her husband, Dennis Revell, after he swore he saw Lincoln standing by the window during one of the couple's overnights in the suite— that is, until she spotted the translucent figure herself during a subsequent stay.

The ghost isn't always visible. Margaret Truman heard knocks at the door that she assumed were Lincoln's. Eleanor Roosevelt often felt she was being watched by an indiscernible someone when she used the room as her study. Others to have sensed the unseen entity in the room were President Eisenhower's press secretary James Hagerty, and the press secretary to Lady Bird Johnson, Liz Carpenter. According to journalist Joan Gage, President Reagan told guests at a 1986 state dinner that his King Charles Cavalier spaniel, Rex, wouldn't stop barking in the empty Lincoln Bedroom. Reagan had the room's wiring checked to make sure the canine wasn't being bothered by a high-pitched electrical frequency. Nothing out of the ordinary was found. Even so, there have also been reports that the lights in the Lincoln Bedroom turn themselves on and off, and cold spots sometimes appear.

Lincoln's ghost hasn't appeared in his namesake bedroom very often since Truman had the suite renovated, but the apparition still occasionally shows up—there and elsewhere in the building. The unmistakable shadowy figure has been observed in the East Room, where Lincoln's body lay in state. In life, Lincoln used the Yellow Oval Room as his library. First Lady Grace Coolidge chanced upon the Illinois Rail Splitter's apparition there, his hands clasped behind his back, staring out the window across the Potomac. Many have seen his silhouette in the same pose; more often, people such as poet Carl Sandburg have "strongly felt his presence" when standing there.

Others to run into Lincoln's spectre in the Executive Mansion include Teddy Roosevelt, Cesar Carrera, President Ford's daughter Susan, and, some say, President Eisenhower, Jacqueline Kennedy, and Lady Bird Johnson. In the 1980s, White House operations foreman Tony Savoy spotted Lincoln's phantom seated in a chair at the top of one of the staircases.

Presidents Theodore Roosevelt, Hoover, and Truman all believed that rapping on their bedroom doors came from Old Abe. (In addition to the knocks and disembodied footsteps in the hall, President Truman also occasionally felt unexplainable cold spots.) Eleanor Roosevelt felt Lincoln throughout the White House, and she thought it was his spirit that caused her dog, Fala, to bark while staring into empty air. Many White House staff members have said off the record that they've heard Lincoln's disembodied footsteps throughout the building. Lillian Rogers Parks confided that she experienced them in the hallway outside the Lincoln Bedroom.

It's unknown how many Lincoln sightings have been true visitations and how many are residual hauntings— what famed ghost hunter Hans Holzer called "transitory impressions." This type of haunting is caused by a person's spirit or essence being impressed on an environment while he or she is still alive, usually during an intense outburst of emotion. Then, after the individual's death, the scene replays itself like a piece of film on a loop. Lincoln certainly experienced enough turmoil in the White House that his aura could have become imprinted on the surroundings.

Besides the stress of being commander in chief during the War Between the States, he had to endure the loss of his eleven-year-old son Willie, who died of typhoid in the Presidential Mansion in 1862.

(Willie's wraith has also been spied in the White House from time to time, beginning in the 1870s by President Grant's staff. President Lyndon Johnson's daughter, Lynda Bird Johnson Robb, then college-age, saw and talked to the little boy as well.)

Remarkably, the Great Emancipator had a vision of his own assassination. Three days before his death, he told his friend Ward Hill Lamon:

> About ten days ago, I retired very late. I soon began to dream. There seemed to be a death-like stillness about me. Then I heard subdued sobs, as if a number of people were weeping. I thought I left my bed and wandered downstairs. There the silence was broken by the same pitiful sobbing, but the mourners were invisible. I went from room to room. No living person was in sight, but the same mournful sounds met me as I passed alone. I was puzzled and alarmed. Determined to find the cause of a state of things so mysterious and shocking, I kept on until I arrived at the East Room. Before me was a catafalque on which rested a corpse wrapped in funeral vestments. Around it were stationed soldiers who were acting as guards; and there was a throng of people, some gazing mournfully upon the corpse, whose face was covered, others weeping pitifully. "Who is dead in the White House?" I demanded of one of the soldiers. "The president," was his answer.

"He was killed by an assassin." Then came a loud burst of grief from the crowd, which woke me from my dream. I slept no more that night; and although it was only a dream, I have been strangely annoyed by it ever since.

On the day of the assassination itself, Lincoln told his personal bodyguard, William H. Crook, that he had been having the portentous dream for three nights straight. Crook tried to talk the president out of attending the play at the Ford's Theatre that evening, but Lincoln refused. He also insisted Crook remain behind. Later, Crook reported that as Lincoln left for the theater he said, "Goodbye, Crook," rather than his customary "Goodnight"—the first and only time he had done so.

It's still debated as to how much interest or belief Abraham Lincoln had in the Spiritualist movement. It's known that Mary Lincoln sometimes invited mediums into the White House to conduct séances, and the president may have attended a few of them. The 1891 book *Was Abraham Lincoln a Spiritualist?*, written by Washington medium Nettie Colburn Maynard, claimed that on February 5, 1863, the president left the safety of the Presidential Mansion to accompany his wife to a séance Maynard conducted in the Georgetown home of Cranston and Margaret Laurie. (The house is still standing. Located at what was once 21 First Street, it's now numbered 3226 N Street NW.)

Lincoln's ghost has been spotted in many places around the country, not just in the White House. One of the first places it was seen was Loudon Cottage in Loudonville, New York. At the time of the assassination, the house was owned by Clara Harris, who was seated in the presidential box at

Ford's Theatre as Mrs. Lincoln's guest. Lincoln also haunts his gravesite in Springfield, Illinois, and each year in April on the anniversary of the passing of the funeral train that carried Lincoln's body (along with that of his son, Willie) from Washington, DC, to Illinois, its apparition materializes along the same sections of track.

Back at the White House, there are other ghosts to be found on the second floor besides Abraham Lincoln. President Howard Taft saw the phantom of Abigail Adams drift through doors to some of the rooms. In the 1940s, as a diplomat and his wife were leaving the mansion after an overnight stay, he confided that his spouse had been frightened by the spectre of a pesky British soldier trying to set fire to their bed several times during the night. Disembodied screams coming from one of the second-story bedrooms are thought to belong to President Grover Cleveland's wife, who was the first to give birth in the Executive Mansion.

During an appearance on *The Tonight Show*, Jenna Bush Hager (daughter of former President George W. Bush) told host Jay Leno that she never saw Lincoln's ghost when she lived at the White House, but there had been a haunted fireplace in her bedroom. One night she woke to hear 1920s music coming out of it. Another evening when her sister stayed with her in the room, they both heard opera music emanating from the fireplace. The next day they asked folks who worked in the White House whether that sounded crazy, but the staff assured them that they heard the music all the time.

Up on the third floor of the White House, hauntings by another former president take place in what was once the attic. William Henry Harrison was the first president to die in office. He also served the shortest number of days.

The sixty-eight-year-old president contracted pneumonia during his inauguration on March 4, 1841, and he died on his thirty-second day in office. If ever there were a candidate for someone who wished to return from the Other Side to complete unfinished business, it would be Harrison. For some odd reason, he's chosen to haunt what in his era was a sloped attic containing storage space and eight small bedrooms for servants. The attic wasn't expanded into a full third floor until 1927, and it's been modernized repeatedly ever since. Nevertheless, Old Tippecanoe (as Harrison was nicknamed) is still heard banging around as if he's looking for something. It's unclear why folks have decided the spectral intruder is Harrison, since his apparition has always remained invisible.

The White House has ghosts from top to bottom: There are even stories about a large "demon cat" hiding out in the basement. (It's uncertain whether the tall tale refers to what is now the ground floor of the Executive Mansion or one of its lower basements.) People who have reported the beastly feline say that when seen from a distance, it appears to be quite small, but as you approach it, the cat disproportionately grows until it's a fearsome size. The creature may not appear for decades; then suddenly there'll be a flood of sightings. The terrorizing tabby is an omen, materializing shortly before a great national disaster or tragedy occurs. The legend is almost identical to claims of a demon cat haunting the halls of the US Capitol. We'll take a closer look at that story in the next chapter.

Finally, there's the Rose Garden on the South Lawn. Dolley Madison planted it prior to her having to flee the White House during the 1814 Burning of Washington, but by a century later it was in poor condition. First Lady Ellen

Wilson ordered the garden be dug up. Workmen tried, but they quit after Dolley's ghost purportedly appeared and chased them away. She didn't want them to tear out her garden. It flourishes today in its original spot and is used as a backdrop for many presidential announcements. Interestingly, the inexplicable aroma of roses is sometimes sensed inside the White House when there are no flowers present.

When asked about the rumors of ghosts in the White House during an appearance on television's *Rosie O'Donnell Show,* then–Secretary of State Hillary Clinton said, "There is something about the house at night that you just feel like you are summoning up the spirits of all the people who have lived there and worked there and walked through the halls. . . . They think there's a ghost there. It is a big old house and when the lights are out it is dark and quiet, and any movement at all catches your attention. . . . It can be a little creepy."

Are the ghosts of Washington, DC, creeping *you* out yet? Well, we're just getting started.

Part Two

CAPITOL HILL

If the focus of the government's executive branch is on the White House, the center of the legislative and judicial branches is Capitol Hill. The small rise, once known as Jenkins Hill, straddles part of the Northeast and Southeast quadrants of the city. To the east is the Anacostia River, to the north is the H Street corridor, to the south are the freeway and the Washington Navy Yard, and to the west is the National Mall.

Everything in L'Enfant's original design for the city fanned out from the Capitol Building. Needless to say, the halls of Congress have their share of ghost legends. But they're far from alone when it comes to hauntings on the hill.

Chapter 2

The Lawmakers

THE CAPITOL BUILDING
1st and East Capitol Streets SE

The legislative branch of the United States government is housed in the Neoclassical-style Capitol Building, which has been in use since the early 1800s. At least twenty phantoms walk its marbled halls.

The US Capitol Building crowning the summit of Capitol Hill is without a doubt the most haunted structure in Washington, DC. Its ghosts may not appear as often as apparitions in some other buildings—a few years at a time may go by without a particular Capitol revenant being seen—but they make the most diverse lot of phantoms in the District of Columbia. There are almost two dozen spectres, many of them identifiable, and they span two hundred years of American history.

The spirits have plenty of places to hide. Labyrinthian halls connect over five hundred rooms, and there are more than sixteen acres of floor space! The Capitol's basic design has been adapted and built upon in several major expansions, so it's almost impossible to grasp the enormity of the building. But in order to get some sense of where the spooks hang out, let's try.

In his original blueprint for the city, Pierre Charles L'Enfant chose Jenkins Hill (now Capitol Hill) as the central hub from which the city would radiate. Congress would be perched atop that rise. It was then–Secretary of State

Thomas Jefferson who insisted the legislative building be named the Capitol (with an "o") after the Latin word meaning "dominant height."

Jefferson solicited competitive designs for the Capitol Building in 1792. A plan by physician and amateur architect Dr. William Thornton was selected. The original design was later modified, as it would be time and again, but President Washington laid the building's cornerstone in 1793. Thornton was named the first Architect of the Capitol, but much of the construction was supervised by James Hoban, who was also busy working on the White House. Thornton was succeeded by Benjamin Henry Latrobe, who put his own touches on the building.

Thornton's layout called for a rectangular central court under a dome with a separate wing on the north and south sides of the building for the Senate and the House of Representatives, respectively. The Senate wing was completed in 1800. The House shared the space until 1807, when it moved into the partially finished south wing. Major work continued there until 1811.

Of course, three years later, on August 24, 1814, the building was partially destroyed when the British set fire to Washington. From 1815 to 1819, Congress met in a temporary structure nearby (later dubbed the Old Brick Capitol) while the actual Capitol Building was being restored. Renovations, which included the addition of the east front portico and a higher dome, continued into the 1820s. The decision was made in 1850 to build extended wings for both the Senate and the House. The latter branch of Congress moved into its new home in 1857; the Senate was able to occupy its wing a few years later. In 1855, work had begun on replacing the existing dome of the Capitol with the Great

Rotunda seen today. A statue named *Freedom* was added to the top of the dome in 1863. By 1892 the building had reached the basic size and shape it is today.

The Capitol Building consists of three levels: the Main floor (which holds offices and the Old Supreme Court Chamber); the Primary or Principal Floor (which includes the Senate Chamber and the Hall of the House of Representatives, the National Statuary Hall, the Old Senate Chamber, and the Great Rotunda); and the Gallery (which contains the balconies of the legislative chambers). Beneath all of this are the massive basement and subbasement, both of which are used for storage.

Originally the Library of Congress was maintained in the Capitol Building, and the US Supreme Court met there as well. Both are now housed in their own structures elsewhere on Capitol Hill. Additional buildings have been constructed to hold the offices of senators and representatives, too. In all, about a dozen buildings now make up the United States Capitol Complex, its most recent addition being the Visitor Center that opened in 2008 off the Capitol's east façade.

Now that we know the basic layout of the land, let's take a look at the Capitol ghosts, one by one, room by room.

We'll start on the first floor in the Old Supreme Court Chamber. The room was designed by Benjamin Latrobe and built in the north wing between 1808 and 1810. Assisting Latrobe was John Lenthall, the Clerk of the Works. The room was located directly below the Old Senate Chamber, and its design—which was radical for its day with vaulted, semicircular ceilings—required new fabrication techniques. Unfortunately, early in the construction, Lenthall removed a wooden support for an archway, thinking it wasn't needed. The brick wall collapsed, crushing him. (Some sources say that Lenthall had argued with Latrobe, saying the support wasn't necessary, and he yanked it out to prove his point.) Legend has it that Lenthall cursed the Capitol with his dying breath—and maybe he did. The epithet is always mentioned when there are problems with renovations to the building.

The first ghost sighting in the Capitol Building started around 1860 in the Great Rotunda on the second floor. The apparition is most likely Robert Slight, a craftsman who died after falling from a scaffold during the construction of the new dome. On the anniversary of the worker's death, his spirit, dressed in coveralls and carrying a wooden tray holding tools of his trade, is seen walking down the hallways heading toward the Rotunda.

A second phantom seen in the Rotunda is a man from the cleaning staff who died while scrubbing its floor. Late at night after the building is closed to tourists, modern maintenance crews hear the sound of his scouring the marble floor and water splashing from an invisible bucket.

Two former librarians haunt the rooms west of the Rotunda that were used to hold the Library of Congress before it got its own building. One of the men is known as Mr. Twine, and his unseen spirit is heard in the corner where his desk was located, stamping the due date on books that congressmen took out on loan. The other librarian hid much of his savings in the pages of the many volumes under his watch, but he died before he could retrieve it or tell anyone where it was. Staff members discovered the cache of almost $6,000 in government bonds when they moved the books across the street to the new Library of Congress building in 1897. Today, the librarian's invisible spectre can be heard frantically flipping through pages of nonexistent books, trying to find his fortune.

Lastly, whenever someone is lying in state in the Rotunda, the spectre of a World War I soldier appears briefly by the coffin and catafalque. He stands at attention, salutes, and then instantly disappears. He's thought to be the spirit of the doughboy who lay in state in the Capitol before being interred in the Tomb of the Unknown Soldier in Arlington, Virginia.

Immediately to the south of the Great Rotunda (after passing through two antechambers) is Statuary Hall. The House of Representatives met there before moving into their new chambers in 1857. In 1864, Vermont Representative Justin S. Morrill proposed that the emptied circular space be turned into an exhibition gallery for statues of notable Americans. Every state has been invited to donate two statues to the Capitol's collection, but due to weight and space limitations, only one from each state is put on display in Statuary Hall.

In the 1890s, a Capitol guard claimed that he walked into the chamber one evening and saw the entire House of Representatives in session, with the room configured the way it had been in the 1850s. A blink, and the ghosts were gone.

Another time, a different night watchman encountered the spectre of Thomas Hart Benton sitting alone at a desk in the middle of the room. Benton, who died in 1858, had been a Senator from 1821 to 1851 before becoming a Representative from 1853 to 1855. That vision, too, evaporated into thin air.

On February 21, 1848, former President John Quincy Adams, then a Representative, suffered a stroke at his desk.

He was taken to the Speaker's Room off the main chamber to recover, but he was too weak to move to a hospital or his home. Adams died there two days later. The remarkable politician was in his ninth term as a Representative after having served as President. At least one Congressional aide standing at the exact spot in Statuary Hall where Adam's desk was located heard muffled whispers that he attributed to the sixth president. Apparently in the evenings, Adams isn't quite so timid. Night staff has heard Adams's booming, disembodied voice denouncing US involvement in the Mexican-American War. (Soldiers' pay was being debated at the time he suffered his stroke.)

Adams is also heard in the former Speaker's Room, which later became the Congressional Ladies Retiring Room. It's said that when it was renamed the Lindy Claiborne Boggs Congressional Women's Reading Room in 1991—the first and only room in the Capitol Building to be named for a woman—Boggs commented, "When they finally gave us a room, wouldn't you know that they'd give us one that was haunted?"

There's a statue of John Quincy Adams in Statuary Hall, and there are those who think it has a glowing translucence, as if there's a spirit lighting it from within. A guard once claimed that at midnight on New Year's Eve all of the statues in the hall came to life, stepped down from their pedestals, and danced. The Capitol policeman was fired—it was thought he may have indulged in a little too much liquid holiday cheer while on duty—but other people have professed the same thing since.

Continuing south from Statuary Hall through a corridor, Capitol visitors come to the Hall of the House of Representatives.

The ghosts of two former Speakers of the House are still arguing in the current House chamber ninety years after their deaths. Joe G. Cannon, a Republican representative from Illinois, served as speaker from 1903 to 1911. Champ Clark, a Democrat from Missouri, held the post from 1911 to 1919. Their long-winded debates from opposite sides of the aisle were legendary. Clark died in 1921, Cannon in 1926, but that hasn't stopped their quarreling. Late in the night, long after work in the chamber has been completed for the day, the sudden rap of a gavel will ring through the air. Both otherworldly orators then materialize on the House floor, and they start to debate anew. Talk about filibusters!

And here's a spooky tale that dates back to 1890. It involves Congressman William Taulbee, who was a representative for Kentucky from 1884 to 1888. His career was ruined when *Louisville Times* political reporter Charles E. Kincaid accused him of committing adultery with a female clerk from the Patent Office. His reputation tarnished, Taulbee never sought reelection, but he stayed in Washington as a lobbyist. His work continued to bring him into contact with Kincaid. Often the ex-congressman would react to Kincaid's continued insults by tweaking his nose or pulling his ear, as if he couldn't be bothered to engage Kincaid in a fight.

On the morning of February 28, 1890, the pair got into a physical tussle, however, as Taulbee was entering the House chamber. Taulbee wound up grabbing Kincaid by the collar and tossing him to one side. Irate and humiliated, Kincaid went home and got a pistol. Around 1:30 p.m. he came up behind Taulbee, who was walking down the staircase from the House chamber to the members' dining room. Kincaid called out his adversary's name; Taulbee turned. The reporter fired, shooting Taulbee under the left eye. The former congressman died eleven days later. Kincaid was charged with murder but pled self-defense. Remarkably, he was acquitted.

A reddish stain resembling blood can be seen to this day on the marble steps where Taulbee was shot. All attempts to remove the ghostly reminder of the murder have been unsuccessful. Staff members say that if a reporter happens to slip on the slick stairs, Taulbee's spirit can be heard laughing. On occasion, Taulbee's phantom briefly appears to gloat! (Some say that the journalists don't fall on their own: Taulbee's ghost trips them!)

Although the legislators' main offices are now in separate buildings adjacent to the US Capitol, the spirits of some departed lawmakers have returned to their working offices and the committee rooms inside the Capitol. From 1858 to 1862, Civil War General John Alexander Logan served in the US House of Representatives as a Democrat for the state of Illinois. After the war, he switched parties and returned to the House from 1867 to 1871. He then served in the Senate from 1871 to 1877 and again from 1879 until his death in 1886. His revenant has returned to the room in the House wing where he used to attend meetings of the Committee on Military Affairs, and he's also been seen strolling through the basement where his stuffed and mounted horse used to be stored.

The apparition of Boise Penrose, a senator from Pennsylvania from 1897 until he died in 1921, was spotted in his old office through the late 1920s.

Wilbur Mills, a Democrat from Arkansas, was one of the House's longest serving representatives, from 1939 to 1977. He died in 1992, but he's still being seen outside his former office—making him one of the Capitol's newest spectres.

Now let's hop all the way back to other end of the Capitol Building, to the Senate wing. There are not a lot of ghost stories connected with the Senate chamber itself, but there's a good one about Henry Wilson, who was a Massachusetts senator from 1855 to 1873. He also served as vice president under Ulysses S. Grant, during the president's second term. Wilson suffered a stroke in May 1873. His health never fully recovered, making his appearances at the Senate sporadic. He died while working at the Capitol in the early morning of November 22, 1875. Wilson's apparition has been seen outside the Vice President's Room ever since. Some sources say the spirit is heard wheezing and sneezing from a cold he caught while bathing in one of the marble tubs kept in the lower floor of the Senate wing for use by the congressmen. Allegedly Wilson's presence in the corridors outside of his former office accounts for the occasional dampness in the air and the scent of soap.

Then there's "Bishop" Sims, who escaped slavery during the Civil War and cut hair for many years in the Senate barbershop on the first floor. He got his nickname from preaching at his church in the Anacostia neighborhood of DC, but at the Capitol he was known for softly singing while cutting the congressmen's hair. Sims died at the age of 93 in 1934, and at some point the barbershop was converted into the House Ways and Means Committee Room. But it's said that people hear Sims yet, crooning gospels in the hallways near the former barbershop.

Perhaps more hauntings take place in the basement than in any other part of the Capitol Building. One of its most regular spectral visitors is the man responsible for literally placing the Capitol on the map: Pierre Charles L'Enfant. Unfortunately, the architect was a headstrong individual who didn't work well with other city planners, so the president reluctantly had to dismiss him.

Congress had not paid L'Enfant for his work up to that point, so the architect spent years trying to collect the thousands of dollars he thought was due him. He finally did receive some money, but by then most of it had to be used to pay his debts. L'Enfant died in extreme poverty in 1825. People say his restless spirit has returned to the Capitol Building and that he's been observed walking the halls, his eyes downcast, muttering quietly, with his city blueprints rolled up under his arm. For some reason, he's been seen most often in the rooms of the basement.

Two of the stonemasons working in the basement on the Senate side of the building in the 1790s got into a heated dispute that turned to violence. One of the men lunged forward with a brick and struck the other mason on the head. The victim was still alive when his assailant sealed him up inside one of the walls. The ghost of the dead stonemason, trowel in hand, now is seen passing through the wall where he was entombed underneath the Old Senate Chamber. (There are several variations to this tale. In some versions, the mason was already dead when he was walled up. Some sources say the dead man's fight was with a carpenter, not a fellow mason. According to others, the murder took place in the Old Senate Chamber, and the hauntings occur there instead.)

On July 2, 1881, a deranged Charles Guiteau shot President James Garfield at the now-demolished Baltimore and Potomac Railroad Station in northwest Washington. Guiteau had convinced himself that he was responsible for Garfield's winning the presidency and was incensed when his bids to be named ambassador to Vienna or Paris were rejected. Garfield didn't die from his wounds immediately, but he never recovered. Instead, he suffered for two agonizing months, passing away later on September 19th, after serious infections, blood poisoning, and, finally, heart failure. Garfield's ghost was seen walking several of the corridors in the Capitol Building while he lay in state in the Grand Rotunda. Guiteau's spectre has appeared in the Capitol Building as well. Back in 1882, a guard spotted Guiteau and, thinking the assassin had somehow escaped prison, chased him down a staircase leading to the basement. Suddenly it dawned on the policeman that Guiteau had already been executed, and in that instant the wraith disappeared.

The basement is also the site of a small chamber that was planned as Washington's Tomb. The room lies two levels directly below the Grand Rotunda, and initially visitors were supposed to be able to gaze down at Washington's sarcophagus from the Rotunda through a glass floor. The tomb wasn't completed until 1827, and in the end Washington's body was never moved from Mount Vernon, where he had been interred in 1799.

For years, Washington's Tomb sat empty. Then it was used to store the catafalque that holds the coffin of those who lie in state in the Rotunda. The ghost of an American soldier from the Revolutionary War materializes in the tomb from time to time, then walks out the room, and vanishes in the hall. Before the catafalque was moved to the new Visitor Center, where it's been put on display, the soldier would encircle the bier before leaving the tomb.

The most common tale of a haunting taking place in the Capitol basement is the frightening appearance of a Demon Cat. The legend is very similar to the story of the fiendish animal said to roam a subbasement of the White House. The fearsome feline was first seen in the Capitol in the early 1800s. There are reports of guards shooting at it in 1862 and 1898, and in each instance the black creature grew to the size of a panther before vanishing.

The Demon Cat is considered to be a bad omen, because it usually shows up immediately before times of national crisis. (For example, it appeared just before the 1929 Stock Market Crash and the assassinations of Presidents Lincoln and Kennedy.) On the other hand, the Demon Cat has been spotted on more ordinary occasions as well. The beast has been glimpsed all over the Capitol Building, but it's most often stumbled upon in Washington's Tomb or prowling the rest of the basement.

Security measures have cut down on the number of rooms visitors can enter in the Capitol Building, but it's certainly worth taking the tour—especially when you consider how many ghosts are wandering the halls. There's no telling who—or what—you may bump into.

Chapter 3

Gone, but Not Forgotten

FORMER SITE OF THE OLD BRICK CAPITOL
1 1ST STREET NE

The apparitions and eerie sounds encountered near the US Supreme Court building in the dark of night have nothing to do with the ghosts of former justices. Rather, they're holdover hauntings from a structure that stood on the site long ago.

If you're standing on the east steps of the Capitol Building facing toward the Visitor Center, there are two monumental buildings directly in front of you. To your right is the Library of Congress, but to your left, on the northeast corner of 1st and East Capitol Streets NE, is the Supreme Court of the United States. The decision-making body has not always met there, however. Construction of the edifice didn't begin until 1932. For more than a century, another structure stood on the spot, and tales of its ghosts and ghoulies echo down to modern times.

The building, called Stelle's Hotel, was a combination inn and tavern made of red brick. Established in 1800, it was located just a few hundred yards from the East Front of the Capitol. It was one of a number of boarding houses in the area that catered to congressmen, their staff, and those who had business with the legislature.

Then came the Burning of Washington in 1814. The Capitol was one of the main targets for the marauding British, and their army left the building in ruins. Congress commandeered Stelle's Hotel, razed it, and built a temporary Capitol Building in its place. Construction was financed by a group of real estate investors who feared that Congress might relocate the nation's capital, which was only two decades old at that point.

The cornerstone for the new building was laid on July 4, 1815, and lawmakers moved in on December 8th. They met there for four years while the original Capitol Building was being restored. After the lawmakers moved back, the interim structure took on a nickname that stuck: the Old Brick Capitol.

With Congress gone, a private school bought the building; then it was broken into apartments and townhouses. Among its tenants was former Vice President John C. Calhoun, who died there in 1850. Calhoun had been a stalwart defender of slavery and states' rights. He didn't promote secession; instead he promulgated the concept of "nullification"—if a state found a federal law to be unconstitutional it could simply declare the act "null and void." According to legend, the ghost of George Washington appeared to Calhoun in the boardinghouse to warn him that his views could lead to the end of the republic.

The outbreak of the Civil War in 1861 changed the building's fortunes. The North needed a place in the capital to house insurrectionists and other political prisoners, members of the military found guilty of insubordination, and POWs—as well as the city's prostitutes, thieves, and other petty criminals. Congress repurchased the Old Brick Capitol and made it the Old Capitol Prison. Some of the other boardinghouses nearby were incorporated into the grounds of the penitentiary. Three of the jail's most famous guests were Confederate spy Belle Boyd and Lincoln coconspirators Mary Surratt and Dr. Samuel Mudd.

During these years, Calhoun's sorrowful spirit was often seen wandering around the prison. Some say the famed politician was bemoaning the toll his beliefs had taken on the country. Others think he was concerned for the comfort of the Confederate inmates, some of whom were merely Southern sympathizers. Cells were overcrowded, mostly unheated during the winter, and sweltering in the summer, but in the middle of the Civil War, Union guards had little inclination to alleviate the conditions.

In 1867, two years after the War Between the States ended, Congress decided it no longer needed the Old Capitol Prison, so it sold the building to George T. Brown, Sergeant at Arms of the US Senate. He reconfigured it into row houses—three separate but connected homes—that collectively became known as Trumbull's Row.

In 1922, the houses were acquired by the National Woman's Party, which had fought for women's suffrage and the passage of the 19th Amendment. Many of the old jail cells were turned into bedrooms and dormitories for its members.

During the NWP's residency, folks living and working in the building heard disembodied voices, including muffled swearing, screams, sighs, and cries, all of which they chalked up to the ghosts of bygone prisoners and soldiers. There were also the sounds of nonexistent cell doors slamming and metal clanging against absent iron bars. Fits of laughter floated through the part of the building where Belle Boyd had been held, and on the anniversary of Mary Surratt's death, her spectre often appeared in the room that had been her cell, even though she had been hanged in the Old Penitentiary at the Washington Arsenal, not in the Old Capitol Prison. Surratt's translucent figure would always be seen crying, standing at the window with her hands clutching iron bars.

People walking outside on the street could occasionally hear the moans and shouts of long-departed detainees coming from inside the one-time jailhouse. In the 1920s, a congressman told of running into the apparition of an ethereal uniformed sentry in front of the building during the predawn hours. The spirit was pacing back and forth guarding the prisoners against rescue or escape.

Finally, in 1929, Congress once again took back the edifice, this time through eminent domain. They leveled it to make way for the construction of the current US Supreme Court Building, which opened in 1935. Up until then, the court had met in the Capitol Building, except for a seven-year period from 1812 to 1819 when it convened outside the city.

Are the hauntings still going on today? The justices of the Supreme Court are notoriously mum about what goes on in the chambers of their citadel, so it's doubtful we'll ever know.

Chapter 4

Bookworm Bogeys

THE LIBRARY OF CONGRESS
10 1st Street SE

FOLGER SHAKESPEARE LIBRARY
201 East Capitol Street SE

Most apparitions are fairly quiet, which makes the library a perfect place for them to hide out. But even when phantoms choose not to show themselves in the stacks, their paranormal activity can make their presence known.

The Library of Congress had humble enough beginnings. Lawmakers provided $5,000 to get it started in 1800 during the administration of John Adams. A separate building didn't exist for it, so the modest collection was set up in a small room in the Capitol.

This made sense at the time, because it was never intended that the public would have access to it. The assortment of books, manuscripts, maps, records, and other documents was assembled to be a reference library for members of Congress. But then came the War of 1812 and the Burning of Washington. The contents of the library were either stolen or went up in smoke when the British looted the Capitol Building and set fire to it in 1814.

Thomas Jefferson, whose presidency had ended five years earlier, offered his personal library to replace the lost holdings. Jefferson's collection was renowned for its size and scope. He had spent fifty years accumulating books that, in his own words, "related to America, and indeed whatever was rare and valuable in every science." He knew that some of the volumes could be considered controversial, because they included foreign-language works and books on philosophy, so he tried to forestall any objections. He pointedly opined, "I do not know that it contains any branch of science which Congress would wish to exclude from their collection; there is, in fact, no subject to which a Member of Congress may not have occasion to refer."

Congress must have agreed, because it paid Jefferson $23,950 for 6,487 books. The collection grew, but in 1851, another fire swept through the library, destroying 35,000 of its 55,000 books. This included two-thirds of the volumes that came from Jefferson, leaving about 2,000 of his books extant. (It's taken 150 years, but the Library of Congress has now replaced copies of all but about 300 of the titles from the Jefferson collection.)

The athenaeum's next great visionary was Ainsworth Rand Spofford, who was Librarian of Congress from 1864 to 1897. He championed the passage of the Copyright Act of 1870, which required publishers to give the Library of Congress two copies of every item being submitted for copyright. In 1871 alone, more than 20,000 books, magazines, pamphlets, engravings, maps, photographs, and sheets of music were added to the library's holdings.

Spofford soon set about convincing Congress that a separate building was needed to house the collection. Lawmakers authorized a design competition in 1873 and, after much haggling, finally agreed in 1886 on an Italian Renaissance plan by two Washington architects, John L. Smithmeyer and Paul J. Pelz. Work on the library began two years later. Located a block to the east of the Capitol Building, it was completed in November 1897.

For the first time, the general public could access the library's books, but it was necessary to view the materials in a supervised reading room. The institution has never been a lending library. Even today, only *very* senior government officials can remove original library materials from the premises.

Herbert Putnam, Librarian of Congress for forty years from 1899 to 1939, worked to make the holdings more available to the public and to other libraries. By the end of his tenure, the Library of Congress was outgrowing what is now known as the Thomas Jefferson Building. Convinced by Putnam, Congress bought a plot on 2nd Street SE in 1928 to build a library annex. Construction began two years later, but because of the Depression the building wasn't finished until 1938. The John Adams Building, as it was named, opened its doors the following year.

The Library of Congress now has a third structure: the James Madison Memorial Building located on Independence Avenue. Librarian of Congress L. Quincy Mumford first envisioned the need for it in 1957, but Congress didn't approve funds for its construction until 1965. It was another six years until ground was broken. The building was essentially completed in 1976, but it wasn't opened to the public until May 1980.

All of the ghosts at the Library of Congress seem to be in the Thomas Jefferson Building. Its most famous unearthly resident is a police sergeant who has been known to help people find their way if they become disoriented in the stacks. Sometimes he appears in uniform; other times, he's in civilian clothes. He seems to be tangible flesh-and-blood, and he'll carry on a conversation with those he meets. It's said that the officer died in the library years ago, and he has returned to the hall as a personal call of duty.

There's also a dark-haired male apparition that meanders through the main building, but his identity is completely unknown. He may or may not be the unseen spirit that thumps on the staircase and opens doors.

There have also been a few never-repeated paranormal occurrences, such as the time painters were working in the north corridor on the second floor of the Jefferson Building. They needed to use a cart that was blocked behind two heavy bookcases. As the men watched, one of the cases moved about a foot, all on its own, to give them enough space to squeeze the cart by.

Today, the national bibliotheca contains in excess of 36 million books and 69 million manuscripts and recordings in more than 450 languages. The collection is second in size only to that of the British Library.

Finally, there also seems to be a ghost at the nearby but non-affiliated Folger Shakespeare Library. Henry Clay Folger, who was chairman of Standard Oil around the turn of the twentieth century, amassed an enormous collection of priceless Shakespeare manuscripts. Seeking a place to hold it, he bought a row of houses on Capitol Street and, in 1928, got Congressional approval to raze the homes so he could build his library. Folger died shortly after the cornerstone was laid two years later, but his wife completed the project. Today the Folger Shakespeare Library holds the world's largest assortment of Shakespeare works, including 82 of the 228 First Folio editions known to exist. It's thought that Folger's phantom has returned to the Reading Room, but he only shows up at night. Evening security guards will turn off the lights as they lock up the room, only to discover that the lights are back on during their next round.

You won't be allowed to conduct a ghost hunt of your own in the Thomas Jefferson Building or the Folger, but their reading rooms are open to the public. If you see something spooky during a visit, remember: Shhh! You're in a library!

Chapter 5

Semper Fi

MARINE BARRACKS
8TH AND I STREETS SE

COMMANDANT HOUSE
801 G STREET SE

OLD HOWARD HOUSE
9TH STREET BETWEEN G AND I STREETS SE

The motto of the United States Marines, Semper Fi, *is short for the Latin phrase "semper fidelis," meaning "always faithful" or "always loyal." Perhaps that's why at least four ghosts have returned to the Barracks.*

Traditionally known as its military branch's oldest post, Marine Barracks is a six-acre complex in Washington, DC, Southeast. President Thomas Jefferson and Marine Commandant Lieutenant Colonel William Ward Burrows personally rode out to find a suitable site that was within easy marching distance to the Washington Navy Yard, the White House, and Capitol Hill. Today, the Barracks take up a full city block, surrounded by G Street to the north, 9th Street to the east, I Street to the south, and 8th Street to the west. (This has led to the compound's nickname: "8th and I.")

Jefferson charged architect George Hadfield with designing and constructing the Barracks, which opened in 1801, along with its Commandant House, which was completed in

1806. The latter three-story home has sixteen-foot ceilings, crystal chandeliers, and several fireplaces but is otherwise not ornately furnished. Located at 801 G Street SE (at the corner of G and I Streets), it's the only surviving original building in the compound; the rest of the structures were replaced between 1900 and 1907. Surprisingly, when the British captured the Marine Barracks after overrunning Washington during the War of 1812, they did not burn down the house.

The entire Marine Barracks, including the Commandant House, was placed on the National Register of Historic Places in 1972 and was named a National Historic Landmark in 1976. The Marine Barracks contains the Corps' official ceremonial grounds and is home to the "President's Own" Marine Band (led for many years by John Philip Sousa, who now haunts Congressional Cemetery) and the "Commandant's Own" Drum and Bugle Corps. Honor guards, funeral escorts, and security forces for Camp David and the White House are among those headquartered at the Barracks.

At least four phantoms make their home at the Marine Barracks. The first, who manifests himself inside the Commandant House, is believed to be the compound's first commandant, Captain Samuel Nicholas. He's not seen, but his disembodied footsteps are heard pacing back and forth in otherwise empty rooms, and residents, staff, and guests have heard the barely audible sound of papers being shuffled about.

No one knows the identity of the second spectre, but she's said to be a little girl who was killed in a car accident inside the lower parking garage. Her ghost sometimes becomes visible, but more often folks passing through the echoing parking structure in the early morning will merely hear the child's cries. Also, a mysterious red ball, thought to have belonged to the youngster, is occasionally seen rolling down one of the ramps.

The last two shadows are part of a great myth at the Marine Barracks. Supposedly, as troops from the Barracks rushed to Bladensburg to fight off advancing British troops in 1814, the payroll for the entire base—hundreds of gold coins in a wooden chest—was entrusted to two Marine sergeants for safekeeping. They did the logical thing: They buried it somewhere on the grounds of the Marine Barracks. The problem is, both men were killed in action, and the treasure has never been found. In the two centuries since, the apparitions of both men have been seen walking the compound, but all attempts to follow them to the fortune have been fruitless. Of course, perhaps they're guarding the money by deliberately leading ghost hunters astray.

There's one more intriguing legend about a spectral Marine, but he didn't live in the Barracks. Instead, in the 1860s, "Old Howard," as the leatherneck was known, took up residence in one of the two-story, wood-frame houses close to 9th and G Streets. The home's exact location is unknown, but there are numerous structures fitting that description in the immediate area.

Old Howard was short-tempered and had frequent violent outbursts. He died in 1871, but his wraith returned and immediately set upon his family. The attacks occurred so often that his widow sold the house and fled with their children after two months.

Subsequent owners—and there were several over the next few decades—had it just as bad, perhaps worse. There were strange knocks coming from within the walls, disembodied groans, and glowing shapes in the dark. Doors would rattle in the middle of the night, but when folks stumbled out of bed to open them, no one was there. Instead, they would be greeted by a hearty laugh. When people were downstairs, they'd hear unexplainable footsteps overhead— and vice versa—and a locked door between the house and an adjacent property would open on its own.

One husband and wife were horrified when the bed they were in was dragged across the room. But their shock turned to shame when the mean-spirited phantom Marine threw open the window and made lewd moaning noises— loud enough to draw the attention of their neighbors.

On one occasion, the eldest daughter of another owner had her bedcovers pulled down by invisible hands, followed by the unseen entity breathing heavily close to her face. Some sources claim the presence crawled into bed next to her.

Old Howard's ghost seemingly preferred to remain invisible, but one person did get a good look his face. It was a servant girl who heard someone climbing the staircase as she lay in bed falling asleep. When she heard a guttural growl by her partially shut door, she opened her eyes to see the jarhead's leering face peeking inside, bathed in the light of the oil lantern he was carrying. As soon as the spectre realized he had been spotted, he shut off the lamp, and streaks of red and blue light began to bounce around the room. The girl's terrified screams awakened the entire household, and everyone dashed out of the building.

Paranormal activity had died down by the mid-1900s, and there have been no recent reports of Old Howard's apparition returning.

Unfortunately, we'll never know if there's a basis of fact in any of these ghost stories. The Marine Barracks can't be visited for obvious security reasons, and Old Howard's house can't be entered, even if it still stands. Pity.

Chapter 6

The Commandant

WASHINGTON NAVY YARD
8TH AND M STREETS SE

It's not every day that a military commander oversees the construction, destruction, and rebuilding of a facility under his care. It's even more unusual for that officer to return after his death to keep his eye on things.

In 1798, Congress recognized the need for an official government agency to oversee the country's naval forces, so it established the United States Department of the Navy, with the Secretary of the Navy being a cabinet-level position. (The naval secretary was a member of the president's cabinet until 1947, when the Department of the Navy was made part of the new Department of Defense.)

President John Adams appointed Benjamin Stoddert the first Secretary of the Navy. (Benjamin Stoddert's ghost is said to revisit his old Georgetown mansion, Halcyon House, but that's a legend for another day.)

America was already involved in the Quasi-War with France when Stoddert took office. Full war was never declared. The conflict mostly consisted of French ships attacking American merchant vessels and the US retaliating against French ships in the Caribbean. The differences between the two nations weren't resolved until 1800.

The hostilities convinced Stoddert that building a strong US battle armada was necessary. In 1799, Congress authorized the purchase of land along the Anacostia River (then known as the Eastern Branch of the Potomac) to build the Washington Navy Yard. The compound's east and north boundaries were 9th and M Streets, respectively. Marshland lay to the immediate west of the base, but it would later be drained and developed. For the next decade, the Navy Yard was the largest naval shipbuilding facility in the country.

In January 1800, Captain Thomas Tingey was asked to supervise its construction. Born in London in 1750, Tingey first entered the British Navy, then later captained merchant ships in the West Indies. He moved to America before the War of Independence, and it's believed he served in the Continental Navy, such as it was. (The American flotilla consisted almost entirely of commandeered British vessels.) His career for the next few decades is sketchy, but in 1798 he led successful raids in the Caribbean as an American captain during the Quasi-War. In 1804, Tingey was made the first commandant of the Washington Navy Yard, and he held that position until his death on February 23, 1829, at the age of seventy-eight. He was buried in the Congressional Cemetery.

But back in 1814, as British troops advanced on the District of Columbia fresh from their victory at the Battle of Bladensburg, Secretary of the Navy William Jones ordered Tingey to do the unthinkable: He was to set the Navy Yard on fire, to destroy and evacuate it before the British could get there—including three warships that were under construction. The Americans could not let their most important naval facility fall into the hands of the enemy!

After the British withdrew from Washington, Tingey oversaw the reconstruction of the Navy Yard. In the ensuing years, the facility's mission changed from shipbuilding to producing ordnance. It had to. The Anacostia River wasn't deep enough to launch the larger battleships required to upgrade the nation's fleet. The yard's focus changed yet again after World War II: to research and technology. Today, the Washington Navy Yard contains offices for a number of naval departments, and it hosts military ceremonies for visiting dignitaries on its large, central parade ground. The base was listed on the National Register of Historic Places in 1973 and was named a National Historic Landmark in 1976.

There are fifteen Officer Quarters located within eight buildings, all of them built in the 1800s. The residences are labeled A through Q, although there is no Quarters I or J. When the Navy Yard opened, most of the senior officers lived in what is now Quarters B. Captain Tingey lived off base in a rented house at 11th and G Streets SE.

In 1804, a two-and-a-half-story, Flemish bond brick house was built for use as the superintendent's home. Its Georgian design is attributed to architect William Lovering. Tingey moved in when he assumed command of the Washington Navy Yard on November 23, 1804. Now the building is officially known as Quarters A, but the place is still popularly referred to as the Tingey House. In 1973, it was separately placed on the National Register of Historic Places, and since 1977 it has housed the Chief of Naval Operations.

The residence sits at the crest of a hill along the North Wall that separates the Navy Yard from M Street. It's a few yards east of the base's Main Gate, the ceremonial entrance designed by Benjamin Latrobe. The house faces Leutze Park (the parade grounds) and has a view of the Anacostia River beyond.

The British didn't bother Quarters A or B when they overran the burning shipyard. The structures were clearly private homes, and the soldiers were only interested in destroying government buildings. Nevertheless, when Captain Tingey returned after the British left the city, he discovered that his house *had* been pillaged—but by his neighbors.

At the time, only a short, wooden fence enclosed the Navy Yard. Nearby residents had crept in and stolen all of the Tingey House's hardware, including doorknobs and many of its doors and windows. (One of the commandant's first acts after his return was to order the construction of a ten-foot wall around the compound.) The house survived the looting and was restored. Over the years, it has been enlarged and significantly altered.

The house is haunted, and the ghost on the second story is Captain Tingey himself! No one's sure why he's returned, much less why he keeps peeking out of the upstairs windows.

According to John Alexander's excellent book, *Ghosts: Washington Revisited,* Tingey had willed the house to his wife, but the government sued to keep it, naturally considering the building to be Navy property. In the end, the Washington Navy Yard prevailed. Maybe the old commandant is still there because he just doesn't take "no" for an answer.

Sometimes legends overlap. Military folklore says that when Marine Commandant Archibald Henderson died in 1859, he also unsuccessfully tried to bequeath his residence at the nearby Marine Barracks to his heirs. Apparently after living in the home for thirty-eight years, he had forgotten that the government owned Commandant House. The apocryphal account differs with the Tingey ghost story in that Henderson's apparition has never come back to stake a claim.

Chapter 7

Dead End

CONGRESSIONAL CEMETERY
1801 E Street SE

EISENHOWER EXECUTIVE OFFICE BUILDING
1650 Pennsylvania Avenue NW

At least three unquiet souls meander among the markers at Congressional Cemetery. With 65,000-plus burials in the graveyard, it's surprising there aren't more. But when the phantoms are as famous as these individuals, three is enough.

Pierre L'Enfant came up with an amazing design for the new national capital, Washington, DC, but his plans didn't include any cemeteries. Recognizing the need for burial grounds, in 1798 the city commissioners suggested two small pieces of land, one at the eastern end of the district and another on the west side. The eastern parcel turned out to be unusable due to frequent flooding, so a group of local residents got together to recommend a better location.

As it turned out, most of those folks were also members of Christ Church in Washington Parish. They picked a 4.5-acre tract along the Anacostia River between E and G Streets and 18th and 19th Streets SE. A deal was worked out in which the church association could sell three-foot-by-eight-foot plots for two dollars each; once they had paid the government the $200 the land cost, the cemetery would become the property of Christ Church. As part of the original agreement, the church would enclose the grounds with a fence, and no "infidels" could be buried there. The debt was repaid and the church received the deed in 1812. In the process, they gave the cemetery a name: Washington Parish Burial Ground.

By that time, a Connecticut senator had died in 1807 and was buried there. Due to the difficulty of transporting human remains over long distances in the nineteenth century, almost every member of Congress to die in office over the next fifty years wound up being interred at that graveyard. As a result, it became known, unofficially, as the Congressional Burying Ground and, eventually, Congressional Cemetery.

In 1820, the church set aside one hundred plots for government use, but Congress wound up buying even more. Lawmakers also provided funds for the graveyard's upkeep and the construction of dozens of cenotaphs (sepulchral monuments in memory of those buried elsewhere) for important political figures who died in office after 1833.

The cenotaphs, clustered near each other in the grave-yard, are identical, plain, block-like markers made of Aquia Creek sandstone, each with a pointed dome. There are plaques on the sides, dedicated to the fallen members of Congress. The shrines were designed by Benjamin Henry Latrobe, second Architect of Congress, who was also responsible for the Decatur House and St. John's Church.

The cenotaph program was ended in 1876, but three more were added in the twentieth century. The only non-Congressional member honored with a cenotaph was William Thornton, first Architect of the Capitol. Today, the federal government owns 806 plots, including about 170 cenotaphs. They're all administered by the Department of Veterans Affairs.

Congressional Cemetery also contains a Public Vault, built between 1832 and 1834 to temporarily hold the remains of prominent government officials until a permanent resting place could be found for them. Among those who were interred in the vault for varying lengths of time were Presidents John Quincy Adams, William Henry Harrison, and Zachery Taylor as well as First Lady Dolley Madison. According to legend, one of the coconspirators in the Lincoln assassination, Lewis Powell, spent a night hiding in the vault after his unsuccessful attempt to kill Secretary of State William Seward.

After the Civil War, many of the cemetery's famous "residents" were disinterred and removed to their home cemeteries, but the graveyard still boasts a vice president, nineteen senators, seventy-one representatives, one Supreme Court justice, veterans from every American war, and former FBI director, J. Edgar Hoover.

None of those political personages roam the property as a ghost. But three other notable Americans do—in order of their deaths, Choctaw Chief Pushmataha, photographer Mathew Brady, and conductor/composer John Philip Sousa.

Little is known of Pushmataha's early life, but 1764 is the generally accepted year of his birth. Beginning at the age of thirteen he fought fiercely against his tribe's Native American enemies, including the Creek, the Osage, and Caddo, often over the diminishing amount of game and fur due to European trappers and traders. In 1800, Pushmataha was made a Choctaw chief, and his logic laced with humor made him a skilled negotiator when he met with US envoys in 1802. In the War of 1812, Native American loyalties split, with some tribes fighting for the British and others for the Americans. Pushmataha wisely backed the latter.

At first, American soldiers referred to Pushmataha as simply "the Indian General," but, as skirmishes against the British continued, their grudging admiration for his leadership and personal exploits grew. Pushmataha was eventually commissioned into the regular US Army, and he was buried with full military honors as a brigadier general.

Pushmataha was no fool. He saw how other Native American tribes were being forced off their homelands and sent westward. Through adroit compromise and treaties with the US he had been able to keep most of his people's traditional lands, which included territory in western Georgia and much of the Deep South.

By the time Pushmataha traveled to Washington in 1824 to discuss yet another cessation treaty, his fellow tribesmen had elected him paramount chief of the Choctaw people. He was especially concerned about settlers encroaching on Choctaw property and the lack of federal enforcement of existing accords. Well respected, he met with President James Monroe, Secretary of War John C. Calhoun, and the Marquis de Lafayette, who was on his last American visit.

During his stay in Washington, Pushmataha developed the croup, which he was unable to shake. On his deathbed, he received a call from his old comrade-in-arms from the War of 1812, Andrew Jackson. Pushmataha was so famous that when he passed on December 24, 1824, newspapers across the country took notice.

Unfortunately for the Choctaw, US expansionists could not be deterred, and in Jackson, who became president in 1829, politicians had a ready ally in their push for Native American relocation. Congress passed the Indian Removal Act in 1830, authorizing the president to offer Native Americans unsettled territory west of the Mississippi in exchange for their lands. In practical terms, the Indians had no choice but to accept. In one of the most sorrowful acts in American history, the Choctaw were forcefully uprooted from their homes and sent to Oklahoma (which was then called Indian Territory). Many were persuaded to walk much of the distance. Between the blizzard of 1831–1832, a cholera epidemic of 1832, and the sheer exhaustion of trying to make such a trip on foot, about 2,500 of the 15,000 Choctaw and 1,000 slaves died on what's become known as the Trail of Tears.

Chief Pushmataha was conciliatory and a compromiser in life, but now that he's in the Next World, maybe he sees how he and his people were betrayed. If so, perhaps it's true what people say: The Indian leader shows his anger and frustration by toppling and breaking tombstones and cenotaphs in the Congressional Cemetery.

Mathew Brady—his first name spelled with one "t"—was born in 1822. He was one of the nation's first professional photographers, having been taught the art of daguerreotype by Samuel B. Morse—who had learned it from Louis-Jacques-Mandé Daguerre himself. (People remember Morse for his eponymous code used in telegraphy; fewer are aware of his work as an artist and portrait painter.) By the end of the 1850s, Brady had switched almost completely to a newer form of photography that was able to produce images on paper from a glass negative.

Among Brady's earliest sitters at his New York photographic studio were Senator Daniel Webster and Edgar Allan Poe. His business was so successful that he opened a second studio in Washington, DC, in 1849. Brady photographed eighteen of the American presidents from John Quincy Adams through William McKinley, missing only

William Henry Harrison. His portraits of Lincoln were used as the model for the president's picture on the penny and the five-dollar bill.

At the beginning of the Civil War, Brady shot hundreds of photos of soldiers who wanted to send them home to their loved ones before going off to battle. He soon decided the war itself should be documented and that he should be the one to do it. Brady got permission from Lincoln to travel to the battlefields and set up mobile photographic studios—with the caveat that it be done at Brady's own expense. Brady assembled a team of at least twenty photographers who traveled to the front lines. (Brady mostly stayed in the District of Columbia and directed his operations from there, although he did venture into the war zones from time to time.)

Few shots were taken of the actual skirmishes, and it wasn't just for safety's sake: Photography at the time required subjects to remain motionless or the image would blur. Instead, Brady's photos showed the aftermath of war: the death and destruction. He and his men also shot hundreds of battlefield portrait shots, both formal and casual. In all, more than 7,000 images were produced, many of them later lost or accidentally destroyed.

As Brady foresaw, the photographs provided an invaluable historical insight into the horrors of war and the magnitude of destruction. In October 1862, Brady exhibited photographs from the Battle of Antietam to a shocked audience: Americans had never seen such graphic images.

The Civil War photographs cemented Brady's place in history. His work also made him the Father of War Photojournalism. But by 1865 the country was war-weary, and demand for exhibitions and the purchase of individual prints dried up. Brady had always thought that the government would buy his collection after the war for their archival value, but Congress had no stomach at the time to authorize the purchase. Even though the War Department had used many of his images during the conflict, they hesitated when it came to purchasing the lot outright—despite the recommendation of senior military officers.

Brady's finances were in ruins. He had spent over $100,000 of his own money to produce the Civil War photographs. In 1875, Congress finally relented and granted Brady $25,000 for some of the collection, but it was too little, too late. By then he had lost his New York studio and most of his clients in DC. Brady's business never recovered.

Then, in 1887, his beloved wife, Julia, died. In 1895, at the age of seventy-three, Brady moved to New York City to prepare a gallery retrospective of his Civil War photos. By then, however, he had Bright's disease, a chronic inflammation of the kidneys. He was living alone, almost destitute, in a New York rooming house when he was struck by a streetcar while out on a stroll. He died in the charity ward of Presbyterian Hospital on January 15, 1896, from his kidney ailment and complications from the accident. Out of gratitude for his service to the country, veterans from the 7th New York Infantry paid for Brady's funeral and burial in Congressional Cemetery.

There are those who believe that a slouching, elderly, bearded man, who walks among the graveyard markers, dressed in a nineteenth-century overcoat and wide-brimmed hat, is none other than Mathew Brady. Others say it's more likely that the photographer's apparition has crossed town, where it's been spotted in the Eisenhower Executive Office Building (EEOB) next to the White House. During Brady's later years in Washington, the EEOB housed the War Department, where he spent many fruitless hours trying to receive compensation for his Civil War photos.

Finally, there's the ghost of John Philip Sousa. Born in Washington, DC, in 1854, Sousa is remembered today as the composer of his many patriotic military marches, including "Semper Fidelis" (the official march of the United States Marine Corps), "The Washington Post," and, of course, "The Stars and Stripes Forever" (which, by a 1987 act of Congress, is the National March of the United States). Often referred to as "the March King," Sousa composed 137 marches, fifteen operettas, eleven suites, five overtures, numerous dances, and hundreds of musical arrangements for others' songs. He is also credited with designing the sousaphone, a refigured helicon (a form of tuba) in 1893.

A child prodigy, Sousa had absolute or perfect pitch and began studying musical composition at six. He apprenticed with the United States Marine Band beginning in 1868, when he was thirteen, and he stayed until 1875. Then, after five years of working with a theater orchestra and learning to conduct, he re-enlisted and returned to the Marine Band as its conductor. He remained in that position for twelve years and had the distinction of leading "The President's Own" band under five chief executives. In 1892, he formed his own band and toured the world. In 1917, despite being 62 years old, he was commissioned as a lieutenant in the United States Naval Reserve during World War I. For two years, he conducted the Navy Band at a naval station in Chicago. He then resumed touring with his own band through 1931.

Sousa died of heart failure in 1932 in Reading, Pennsylvania. He was seventy-seven. A legend in his own time, the grand bandmaster was buried in a family plot in the southwest corner of Congressional Cemetery.

Each year on November 6th, the anniversary of Sousa's birth, the Marine Corps Band visits their illustrious former leader's gravesite and plays a tribute at his tomb. But then there's the *other* music: On moonless nights, folks sometimes hear the unexplainable brassy, bass sounds of an ethereal sousaphone emanating from the general area where the March King is interred.

Over the last century, Congressional Cemetery has grown to encompass 35.75 acres. It entered the National Register of Historic Places in 1969 and was named a National Historic Landmark in 2011. It continues to be an active, privately owned burial ground, managed by the Association for the Preservation of Historic Congressional Cemetery. If you haven't made your final arrangements yet, why not consider moving in? Perhaps one day you could join its Ghostly Trio.

Part Three

LAFAYETTE SQUARE

In L'Enfant's original design, a large President's Park completely surrounded the Executive Mansion. In 1804, President Thomas Jefferson allowed Pennsylvania Avenue to extend through the park for easier access to the White House. This created a seven-acre square in front of the mansion bordered by H Street on the north, Madison Place on the east, and Jackson Place on the west. The space was officially dubbed Lafayette Park in 1824 in honor of the Marquis de Lafayette.

In the city's first few years, the area was used variously as a soldier encampment, a slave market, and a graveyard. But due to its proximity to the White House, the square soon became a fashionable address for society—and several of its early residents are said to remain there, haunting what's been called "Tragedy Square."

Chapter 8
Hello, Dolley!

CUTTS-MADISON HOUSE
1520 H Street NW

Dolley Madison may have done more to define America's notion of a First Lady than any other occupant of the White House. The phrase "life of the party" doesn't do her justice: She's still entertaining visitors, even after her death.

Few figures from the early years of Washington, DC, are more fascinating than Dolley Madison, the wife of James Madison, fourth president of the United States. She was born Dolley Payne into a Quaker household in North Carolina in 1768, the eldest daughter of John Payne Jr., a plantation owner, and his wife, Mary Coles Payne.

Let's get the question about the spelling of her first name out of the way. Her name was registered at birth with her parents' Quaker fellowship as "Dolley," although some people at the time may have also used the spelling "Dollie." Her last will and testament begins "I, Dolly P. Madison," and the usage "Dolly" was frequently seen in nineteenth-century periodicals. A biography written by her grandniece in 1896 used the spelling "Dolly" throughout the book. Nevertheless, modern scholarship seems to favor "Dolley."

Dolley Payne moved with her family to Virginia, then on to Philadelphia. There, she married John Todd, a lawyer, in January 1790, and they had two sons. A yellow fever epidemic in 1793 killed both her husband and the younger boy.

It's possible that, by that point, she had already met James Madison at social events in Philadelphia, where Madison was a Virginia Representative in Congress. In May 1794, Aaron Burr (Madison's friend since their college days together) formally introduced the twenty-six-year-old widow to Madison, a forty-three-year-old bachelor. A whirlwind courtship followed, and they married in September. They remained in Philadelphia until 1797, at which time Madison left politics and moved back to Montpelier, his family plantation in Virginia.

Madison's retirement was short-lived. When Thomas Jefferson became president in 1800, he called on Madison to be his secretary of state. James, Dolley, Dolley's son, Payne, and Dolley's sister, Anna, moved to the new federal capital and set up house. Dolley instinctively understood that, as the wife of a cabinet member, her duties would include entertaining visitors, and she did so with panache.

In addition to greeting guests in her own home, Dolley also assisted President Jefferson at the White House. Jefferson's wife, Martha, had died in 1782, so Dolley was sometimes called on to act as the hostess at galas, formal banquets, and the like. (This experience would serve her well when she became a first lady herself.) Jefferson also asked Dolley to advise on furnishing the interior of the presidential mansion.

Madison was elected to succeed Jefferson, and he served two terms, including the tumultuous period of the War of 1812 and the Burning of Washington. The president was observing the front lines as the British approached the capital in late August 1814. After witnessing the enemy's victory at the Battle of Bladensburg, Madison sent back word that his wife and their entire staff had to evacuate the city. It's said that Dolley Madison refused to leave the White House until Gilbert Stuart's full-length portrait of George Washington was taken down and secure. After the war, the legend arose that Dolley had personally removed the picture from its frame, making her a beloved heroine.

A few days after the British left the city, Dolley returned to Washington to meet her husband. The White House was ravaged. Colonel John Tayloe offered the Madisons his home, Octagon House, to act as the Executive Mansion until the White House was restored. They accepted the magnanimous offer, and they lived in the Octagon House until Madison left office in 1817.

After that, the couple returned to Montpelier, where Dolley continued to welcome guests into her home. At one point she wrote, "I am less worried here [at Montpelier] with a hundred visitors than with 25 in W[ashington]."

James Madison died at his plantation in 1836 and was buried in the family cemetery on the property. Dolley remained at Montpelier for a year, organizing her husband's papers. Congress granted her $55,000 to prepare seven volumes of them for publication, including Madison's diaries, which detailed the debates that took place at the 1787 Constitutional Convention.

In 1837 Dolley returned to Washington along with her butler, Paul Jennings, and her niece, Anna Payne. She left Montpelier in the hands of her son, John Payne Todd. Dolley moved into a gracious house located on Lafayette Square that was owned by her sister Anna and her husband, Richard Cutts.

The three-story, Federal-style building was constructed in 1822. Cutts had placed the front door to his home facing the square at 721 Madison Place NW, and Dolley often sat in a rocking chair on a small porch running along part of the first floor façade.

Unfortunately, Dolley's last years were not carefree. In fact, she faced extreme financial difficulty. Her son, an alcoholic whom she and her husband had rescued from debtor's prison in 1830, was unable to run the plantation profitably. To pay her debts, Dolley was forced to sell, first, her butler, then several other slaves, followed in 1844 by Montpelier and its furnishings. (Jennings was purchased by Daniel Webster, who allowed him to earn his way to freedom.) Dolley was near destitute in 1848 when Congress bought James Madison's remaining papers for either $20,000 or $25,000. (Sources vary.)

Dolley Madison died the next year at the age of eighty-one at the Cutts-Madison House, now more popularly known as the Dolley Madison House. Initially she was buried in the Public Vault in the Congressional Cemetery on Capitol Hill. Her remains were later moved to the Cutts vault, but in 1858 she was reinterred next to her husband at Montpelier.

In his eulogy, President James Taylor called Dolley Madison "the first lady of the land for a century," perhaps the first usage of that phrase. Regardless, it stuck, and the term "first lady" has been used to describe the role of every president's wife since.

In 1851, Rear Admiral Charles Wilkes purchased the Cutts-Madison House. He moved the entrance to H Street NW, which accounts for its current address, and he took down the porch on the west side of the building.

Sightings of Dolley Madison's ghost began shortly after her death. She would appear at her Lafayette Square home, rocking in her chair on the porch, then later in the space where it had been. Her visitations were so frequent that gentlemen attending the nearby Washington Club, then the city's most prominent men's social club, would often tip their hats to Dolley as they passed by.

Dolley's spectre doesn't stick to her former house on the square, however. She has appeared to workers in the White House Rose Garden, which she planted prior to the War of 1812. The ghostly scent of its flowers are sometimes detected inside the White House, even when the roses aren't in bloom. Dolley's spirit is also seen periodically in the Octagon House.

Today, a small plaque on the outside of the yellow house at the corner of Madison and H Streets reminds people of its most famous occupant. The building isn't open to visitors, but it doesn't need to be. On tranquil nights, a smiling, elderly lady is sometimes seen outside, rocking away. If you're on a late-night stroll in Lafayette Square, pause. Take a peek. Perhaps you'll catch a glimpse of the phantom first lady.

Chapter 9

Ready, Aim, Phantom

DECATUR HOUSE
1610 H Street NW

Even a war hero's life can come to an unhappy end. Such was the case for Stephen Decatur, America's most celebrated naval commander from the First Barbary War. Perhaps it's Decatur's pointless death that's led to his spirit's unrest.

When Stephen Decatur Jr., moved to Washington, DC, with his wife, Susan, in 1816, he decided to build his residence close to the White House. The three-story, nearly square, red-brick, Federal-style home was constructed at the northwest corner of President's Park, which is known today as Lafayette Square. (The front door opened onto 748 Jackson Place NW, but its official address is now 1610 H Street NW.) The house was built in 1818, and the Decaturs moved in the following year.

Decatur was still in his thirties, but he was already famous from his exploits during the War of 1812. Many politicians at the time believed that, if Decatur's ambitions ran in that direction, he could one day become president. And perhaps they did. No doubt Decatur was well aware of the importance of having friends in high places when he chose the location for his house and asked architect Benjamin Henry Latrobe to design a home that was "fit for entertaining." As soon as the Decaturs settled in, they began to throw a series of elegant parties for Washington society.

Decatur's choice of Latrobe was no accident either. Latrobe was a noted British neoclassical designer and one of the most famous and politically-connected architects of the day. As the second Architect of the Capitol, Latrobe oversaw the Capitol Building's completion. He also designed St. John's Episcopal Church on Lafayette Square, the main gate of the Washington Navy Yard, and the porticos of the White House.

Stephen Decatur Jr., was born in Maryland on January 5, 1779. His father was an officer in the navy during the War of Independence. Young Decatur, wishing to follow in his father's footsteps, joined the navy at nineteen. He was a quick study. Indeed, in 1799 President Adams promoted the young man to the rank of lieutenant.

Decatur served with merit during the Quasi-War with France, but his true fame came from an exploit during the First Barbary War. The American Navy was trying to stop pirates who were raiding vessels off the coast of North Africa. On Halloween 1803, the USS *Philadelphia* became stuck on a reef near Tripoli, and Decatur came up with a daring scheme to try to recover it. By then he was in command of the *Intrepid*. He had his ship disguised as a Maltese merchant ship, and with an eighty-man volunteer crew, sailed into Tripoli harbor claiming his ship needed to make repairs. They anchored next to the *Philadelphia* and attempted to free it. When it proved impossible to move the vessel, Decatur followed orders and set the *Philadelphia* ablaze rather than let the enemy repair it and add it to their own fleet. The *Intrepid* escaped with no men lost.

Decatur was immediately lauded as a hero for the success of his mission. Largely as a reward, he was made a full captain in February 1804. At the age of twenty-five, he was the youngest American ever to receive that rank.

Decatur continued to serve valiantly through the remainder of the Barbary War. Then, in 1806 with the nation at peace, he married Susan Wheeler, the daughter of the mayor of Norfolk.

If all this seems more history lesson than ghost story, there's a reason: Decatur's meteoric rise was cut short by his untimely death from a duel, and it may be "unfinished business" that compels his spirit to return.

A dress rehearsal for Decatur's fatal encounter had come back in 1799 when he was in Philadelphia recruiting crew for the USS *United States*. A chief mate from an East India Company ship made slanderous remarks about Decatur and the US Navy. Unable to receive an apology, Decatur challenged the man to a duel. Decatur knew he was a better shot than the chief mate, however, so on the dueling grounds he deliberately shot his opponent in the hip rather than aiming to kill. Both men left with honor—and, more importantly, they were both alive.

Decatur's next duel would not end as well.

In 1807, a British ship, the HMS *Leopold,* chased down the USS *Chesapeake* off the coast of Virginia. The American vessel was under the command of Commodore James Barron. The English captain demanded Barron turn over three sailors, claiming that the men were deserters from the British military. When the commodore refused, the *Leopold* engaged the *Chesapeake* in battle. Having just set out to sea, the US ship wasn't prepared to return fire. There was heavy damage to the *Chesapeake*, three of its men were killed, and another eighteen were wounded. In the end, Barron surrendered the ship. The British boarded it, took the three men they wanted, and, having no other interest in the American vessel, released it. The *Chesapeake* limped back to port.

In the subsequent inquiry, Barron was court-martialed, relieved of command, and given a five-year suspension. Decatur served on the board that passed down the sentence and was particularly critical of the commodore's actions during the hearing. As a result, Barron blamed Decatur most for the loss of his commission, and he was further enraged when, days later, Decatur was given command of the *Chesapeake*.

Barron knew Decatur well. They had served together as lieutenants on the *United States* in 1800, and Decatur had served as first lieutenant under Commodore Barron on the USS *New York* in 1802.

After the court martial, Barron and Decatur exchanged a number of heated letters, with escalating insults and threats coming from Barron. Finally, in March 1820, Barron challenged Decatur to a duel. Decatur felt a need to defend his honor and feared a loss of respect if he refused. After much soul searching, he reluctantly agreed.

In the early-morning hours of March 22, 1820, Decatur slipped out the back door of his house without telling his wife and made his way to a popular dueling ground six miles away in Bladensburg, Maryland. The rivals met promptly at nine o'clock. Decatur had agreed that the duel could be fought at a distance of eight paces instead of the usual ten because Barron was near-sighted. The rules stated that once the foes turned to face one another, they could fire as soon as the count of "one" but no later than the count of "three."

Both men fired at the same time; both were hit. Barron was struck in the right hip, but the ball that hit Decatur lodged in his stomach. Decatur immediately clutched his side and cried, "Oh, Lord, I'm a dead man." He was right. Barron, the provocateur, survived the duel, but Decatur, who was rushed back to his home on Lafayette Square, died at 10:30 that evening on the first floor of his house.

Decatur had lived in his new home for only fourteen months. After his death, Decatur's widow moved to Georgetown and rented out the Lafayette Square house for the next fifteen years. From 1827 to 1833, the house was leased, in succession, by Henry Clay, Martin Van Buren, and Edward Livingston, all of whom served as secretary of state at the time they lived there.

In 1836, Susan Decatur sold the house to John Gadsby, who owned the National Hotel on Pennsylvania Avenue and, for many years, Gadsby's Tavern in Alexandria, Virginia. After Gadsby's death in 1844, his widow, Prudence, rented the property to a litany of politicians and businessmen, including Vice President George M. Dallas. The federal government acquired the building next. During the Civil War, it was turned into offices for the US Army. Then, in 1872, after six years with no occupants, the Decatur House was bought by Edward Fitzgerald Beale, a colorful frontiersman-turned-diplomat. He and his wife, Marie, furnished the interior in Victorian style, added gas chandeliers, and placed parquet floors in the second-floor parlors. Eventually, Beale's daughter-in-law, Marie, inherited the house, and in 1956 she willed it to the National Trust for Historic Preservation. In the early 1960s, the residence was opened as a museum. Although the modern renovations were retained on the house's upper floors, the first floor has been restored to its original nineteenth-century appearance. In 1976, Decatur House was designated a US National Landmark.

The building has been haunted for almost a century. Sightings of Stephen Decatur's ghost began there almost immediately after his death. Often his phantom would appear in his bedroom, or passersbys would see his melancholy spirit staring out of a second-story window overlooking H Street. Others have reported feeling an overwhelming sadness when standing in the room in which Decatur died. Folks outside the house have spotted Decatur's spectre carrying a box of pistols as it passes through the same rear door he exited that fateful morning. Susan Decatur died in 1860 at the age of eighty-four. Since that time, a number of people have heard her invisible spirit sobbing inside the house.

Today, the Decatur House museum is operated by the White House Historical Association. Why not pay it a visit? It's the patriotic thing to do. Besides, you might wind up meeting the ghost one of America's first great naval heroes.

Chapter 10

The Woebegone Wife

HAY-ADAMS HOTEL
800 16TH STREET NW

ROCK CREEK CEMETERY
201 ALLISON STREET NW

In ghost folklore, it's not unusual to hear of a suicide who returns to roam the earth. What's more unusual is the phantom showing up in a place the person never visited while alive—which is what makes this exception to the rule all the more fascinating.

An inconsolable spectre roams the passageways of the five-star luxury Hay-Adams Hotel in Washington, DC. The female apparition was never a guest. In fact, she never stepped foot inside. But her emotional connection to the ground on which the hotel stands is, perhaps, an even stronger magnet drawing her back.

The story begins in 1872 when Marian "Clover" Hooper married Henry Brooks Adams, a critically acclaimed American novelist, journalist, historian, and Harvard professor. He also happened to be the grandson of John Quincy Adams, the sixth president of the United States and a descendant of the second president, John Adams. As for Marian, she was so vivacious that many believe she was the inspiration for the title characters in Henry James's novels *Daisy Miller* (1878) and *The Portrait of a Lady* (1881).

Henry and Clover moved to DC in 1877. They rented the Slidell House at 1607 H Street NW on the north side of Lafayette Square. The couple invited politicians, academics, and socialites to their home to create the kind of salon that would only be possible in a world capital.

During this period, the couple became particularly close to John Hay and his wife, Clara. Soon, the Hays were holding soirees as well. John Hay had been a personal secretary to President Abraham Lincoln and served as secretary of state under both William McKinley and Theodore Roosevelt. Like Adams, he was also an author.

The Hay-Adams circle expanded to include a fifth host, the distinguished geologist Clarence King. Before long, the group called themselves the "Five of Hearts" and had custom china and letterhead stationery made bearing the sobriquet. Their elegant evenings of sophisticated conversation continued through the administrations of three presidents—Rutherford B. Hayes, James Garfield, and Chester A. Arthur. Among the many guests they welcomed to their doors were Teddy Roosevelt, Mark Twain, Henry James, and sculptor August Saint-Gaudens.

In 1881, Adams purchased property on the northwest corner of 16th and H Streets so that he and Hay could build adjacent houses. They hired Henry Hobson Richardson as their architect. Both homes were designed in a Romanesque style, and construction started first on the Hay residence.

Marian Adams became interested in photography around 1883, and her portraits were remarkable for their day. Like most photographers then, she personally developed the negatives and made prints in her own darkroom. She also kept detailed notes about the processes she used. Her work was good enough that she could have entered the field professionally, but her husband dissuaded her. As a result, most of her images were never published during her life-time. (Today the negatives and many prints are housed at the Massachusetts Historical Society in Boston.)

In April 1885, Marian's father died. She had been deeply—even obsessively—devoted to him, and over the next several months she struggled with severe depression. Unable to shake her loss, Marian Adams committed suicide on a Sunday in early December 1885 by swallowing potassium cyanide, one of the chemicals she used to develop photos. She was forty-two. Her husband found her lifeless, lying on the rug in front of her bedroom fireplace. It being a gentler time, the newspapers reported she had died from paralysis of the heart rather than create a scandal.

Henry Adams was devastated. He destroyed all of his letters from Marian, seldom spoke of her again publicly, and never mentioned her in his autobiography, *The Education of Henry Adams*. He commissioned Saint-Gaudens to create a sculpture to mark her grave in Rock Creek Cemetery, asking him to draw inspiration from Buddhist art. The result was a bronze, shrouded and robed, androgynous figure named *The Mystery of the Hereafter and The Peace of God that Passeth Understanding*. Most people refer to the statue as *Grief*.

The sorrowful, seated figure is positioned in front of a granite wall as part of the overall Adams Memorial designed by Stanford White. It's said the statue is so unsettling that, at first, the cemetery wasn't going to allow it to be placed there. The artwork has stood the test of time, however. In 1972, the Adams Memorial was placed on the National Register of Historic Places. In time, the hexagonal burial plot also became the final resting place of Henry Adams. Legend has it that Marian Adams's phantom sometimes appears hovering or standing near her grave.

Clover didn't live to see the completion of her new home, but that's not to say her spirit never visited it. Some say Henry Adams became more reclusive in his later years because his wife's ghost had returned to haunt their house! Next-door neighbors even claimed they sometimes heard a woman's voice wailing and sobbing inside.

John Hay died in 1905. When Clara passed away in 1914, their daughter, Alice, and her husband, Senator James Wadsworth, inherited the Hay house. The couple bought the Adams property after Henry died in 1918 and later leased it to the Brazilian Embassy.

Rumors of Clover's ghost continued throughout this entire period. Some said there was a perennial cold spot in front of the fireplace where Marian's body was discovered. Her spectre sometimes appeared in a rocking chair in that same bedroom. She would lock eyes with anyone who spotted her, causing the person to be overcome with despair or to scream. At that point, the phantom would disappear.

In 1927, a Washington, DC–based developer named Harry Wardman bought the Hay and Adams houses and tore them both down. In their place he built a 138-room luxury hotel. In a nod to the original residences, he named his new accommodations the Hay-Adams Hotel and used some of the paneling from the Hay house in one of the hotel's public spaces, the Hay-Adams Room.

Designed in the Italian Renaissance style by Mirhan Mesrobian, the Hay-Adams Hotel cost an astounding $900,000 when it opened in 1928. It had every modern convenience a well-heeled guest could have asked for, including steam heat, ice water on tap, elevators, suites with kitchens, and, beginning in 1930, air conditioning in the dining room. Early guests included Charles Lindbergh, Amelia Earhart, Sinclair Lewis, and Ethel Barrymore.

In addition to all the amenities, the hotel also soon had a ghost: Clover Adams!

From the beginning, there have been whispers that an invisible female spirit can be heard crying in a room or a stairwell. Sometimes it would ask, "What do you want?" Most of the visitations take place on the fourth floor, and they occur most frequently during the first two weeks in December—around the anniversary of Marian's death.

There are other phenomena as well. Locked doors open and shut on their own. Radios turn on and off by themselves. Housekeepers have heard an unseen woman call them by name. Now and then, the phantom hugs them! The ghost causing all the commotion has never been seen, but the paranormal activity is often accompanied by the scent of mimosa (Marian's favorite aroma) and, more specifically, almonds (an odor shared with potassium cyanide).

The Hay-Adams Hotel was purchased in the 1933 by Julius Manger, the largest independent hotel operator in the United States at the time. He moved into the Hay-Adams and lived there until his death in 1937. The hotel stayed in the family until 1973, during which time it was known as the Manger Hay-Adams. The hotel was completely renovated in 2001, and five years later the B. F. Saul Company, a Washington real estate firm, bought it for a reported $100 million. The hotel made the news in 2009 when president-elect Barak Obama and his family stayed there for two weeks prior to his first inauguration. The Hay-Adams made additional upgrades in 2010 and 2011. The hotel now boasts 145 rooms and 20 suites.

Meanwhile, Clover Adams lives on. Her spirit can still be encountered at the Hay-Adams Hotel off Lafayette Square. What better reason for an overnight stay?

Chapter 11
O Say, Can You See

SITE OF THE PHILIP BARTON KEY SHOOTING
Lafayette Square

A man who enters an affair with a married woman has to be aware there could be consequences, especially if he's the US district attorney. What Philip Barton Key never suspected was that the repercussions from his indiscretions might turn out to be deadly.

Sex scandals are nothing new to the District of Columbia!

Although the name Daniel Sickles is now mostly forgotten, he was one of the most celebrated, well-connected, and controversial men in Washington in the middle of the nineteenth century. Born in New York City in either 1819 or 1825 (during his lifetime, he gave both dates), Sickles studied law. He was elected to the New York State Assembly in 1847, and five years later, he married the teenage Teresa Bagioli. (Sources state her age variously from fifteen to seventeen.) After a stint as a corporate counsel for New York City, Sickles was appointed by President Pierce to serve as secretary to the US diplomatic legation in London, which was led by James Buchanan. Sickles returned to America and served two years as a member of the New York State Senate before being elected to the US House of Representatives in 1857. (During that same election, he actively campaigned for Buchanan, who won the presidency.)

Clearly, Sickles had "friends in high places." This had served him well, allowing him to ride through a series of scandals that would have ended many other politicians' careers. Sickles was a known womanizer, for example. He had also welcomed a notorious prostitute, Fanny White, into the New York Assembly chambers. He then took her on a "business trip" to London and presented her, under a pseudonym, to Queen Victoria while leaving his pregnant wife at home. But none of these shenanigans compared to his actions after he discovered Teresa was having an affair with Philip Barton Key II.

Key, named for his great-uncle, was the US attorney for the District of Columbia and also happened to be one of the sons of Francis Scott Key, the author of the lyrics for "The Star Spangled Banner." The lawyer was a forty-one-year-old widower, handsome, and, like Sickles, a ladies' man. The two men knew each other well. Besides being in politics, both were members of the Washington Club, the most prestigious men's social club in the city. It was located on Madison Place in the southwest corner of Lafayette Square.

Whether Sickles was increasingly away for work or simply chose to spend less time at home is uncertain, but Key began to escort Teresa Sickles to a number of functions around town. Even the society pages of the newspapers took note. Gossip soon started to spread that the couple had become involved romantically, and the rumors were not unfounded. Key rented a home on 15th Street very close to the Sickles residence on Lafayette Square, and the young wife would often slip over to her lover's house—but not as discreetly as she believed. Before long, their relationship was an open secret; everybody seemed to know about it but Daniel Sickles.

Finally, someone slipped Sickles an anonymous note, tipping him off about the affair. Once he had confirmed from friends that the charge was true, Sickles rushed home to confront his wife. She admitted her infidelity and later that evening wrote out a detailed confession, which two people witnessed her sign.

On Sunday, February 27, 1859, as Key strolled by the Sickles house on his way to the Washington Club, he signaled Teresa by waving a handkerchief at her window, totally unaware that the affair had been discovered. The fluttering hanky caught Sickles's attention, and he stormed out of the house and ran toward Key. He caught up to him in the middle of the park, drew a pistol, and fired. The bullet merely grazed Key. Sickles raised the gun again, but the unarmed Key managed to knock it out of the assailant's hand. Sickles pulled out a second pistol and again fired at Key, this time striking him on the upper thigh. Key fell backward against a tree. Sickles drew closer, aimed the derringer point blank at Key and—click—the gun misfired. Key begged for mercy as Sickles calmly reloaded, leveled the gun at Key's chest, and fired. This time, he was successful, mortally wounding Key. Sickles stood over his rival's body, pressed the gun against Key's head, and tried to shoot him again. The gun failed to go off, but Sickles, satisfied, stepped away.

Key was bundled up by several men and carried off to the home of Benjamin James Tayloe, whose father, Colonel John Tayloe III, had built the nearby Octagon House. The son's residence was located on Lafayette Square at 21 Madison Place between the Washington Club and the Cutts-Madison House. Key died in the Tayloe House a short time after being taken there.

Key was interred thirty miles away at the Westminster Burial Ground in Baltimore, Maryland. But his spirit didn't stay there. Instead, his phantom is seen wandering Lafayette Square, most often close to the spot where he was gunned down. Key's spectre also ambles along 15th Street, where he was living at the time of his death. (Legend has it that his ghost also saved the life of President Lincoln's secretary of state, William Seward, but more about that in a moment.)

So what happened to Sickles? Well, he didn't resist arrest. Immediately after the shooting he walked the few blocks to the home of Attorney General Jeremiah Black and confessed to the crime. Sickles was allowed a short visit to his home and was then taken to jail. The public was largely sympathetic to Sickles. He was given extraordinary privileges in prison, and a number of leading politicians and members of society visited him. Even President Buchanan sent a note of support.

A cadre of top lawyers including James T. Brady, a product of New York's Tammany Hall, and Edwin M. Stanton, who would later become secretary of war, represented the murderer at trial. Sickles pled temporary insanity—the first time the defense was used in the United States—and the strategy was successful.

Found not guilty, Sickles withdrew from the public eye for a time, but he didn't resign from Congress. Then, at the start of the Civil War, he returned to New York to recruit volunteers for the Union Army. He was made colonel of one of the regiments, and by 1863 he had risen in the ranks to become a major general. At the Battle of Gettysburg, his superior, Major General George Meade, ordered Sickles to take up a defensive position on Cemetery Ridge, but Sickles disobeyed the command and deliberately moved his corps almost a mile closer to the enemy.

When the Confederates attacked on July 2nd, Sickles's men bore the brunt of the assault. Historians debate whether Sickles's maneuver may have inadvertently prevented the capture of Cemetery Ridge and Cemetery Hill by diverting the Confederate attack. In any event, Sickles was hit in the right leg by a cannonball during the battle, and the limb had to be amputated later that day. He immediately returned to Washington, DC, and was one of the first to let Lincoln—and the press—know about the victory at Gettysburg.

Charges of insubordination were never filed against Sickles. In fact, he was eventually awarded the Medal of Honor. He remained in the army until 1869, after which he accepted several appointed offices, including US Minister to Spain from 1869 to 1874—where he may have had an affair with the deposed Queen Isabella II. By that point, however, his wife, Teresa, whom he had purportedly forgiven, had died.

Sickles passed away in 1914 at the age of ninety-four and was buried in Arlington National Cemetery. One of his legacies was his crusade to make Gettysburg Battlefield a national military park. Among other contributions, he was responsible for moving the fencing that surrounded Lafayette Park to East Cemetery Hill to mark the border of the conflict.

On a macabre side note, at the time of the amputation of his leg, Sickles was aware that the army surgeon general had made a request for commanders in the field to send him "specimens of morbid anatomy . . . together with projectiles and foreign bodies removed" for study and display at the recently opened Army Medical Museum. Sickles sent his leg, and the shattered bone was put on exhibition next to a cannonball similar to the one that struck it. Sickles supposedly went to see his severed limb each year on the anniversary of its removal.

According to some people, visits by Sickles didn't stop with his death. Even though the museum has changed locations a few times, night guards have occasionally seen the shadow of a one-legged, obese man resembling Sickles in his later years pass by the cabinet where his bones were laid out. But perhaps he's grown tired of the vigil. The leg has been at the National Museum of Health and Medicine in Fort Detrick, Maryland, since May 2011, but there have been no reports there of Sickles's ghost.

The building that housed the Washington Club on Lafayette Square is long gone. The three-story brick house was constructed in 1830 as a residence for Commodore John Rodgers. It then briefly became home to a succession of politicians, including Henry Clay and John C. Calhoun. The Washington Club occupied the property next, but it once again became a private home when Secretary of State William Seward moved in around 1861.

On the night of the Lincoln assassination, coconspirator Lewis Powell (also seen as Lewis Paine or Payne) broke into the Seward mansion to kill the secretary. Seward would have been easy prey: He was bedridden from injuries he had sustained in a carriage accident. But Seward was saved by a loud, unusual, and utterly unrecognizable noise. The commotion alerted his son and a manservant, who arrived almost immediately and were able to fend off the intruder. Powell managed to escape, and Seward survived the attack. Most people assume Powell was simply inept and had caused the clamor himself. Paranormalists believe that Philip Barton Key, unwilling to allow another murder to take place in Lafayette Square, produced the warning.

Seward's invalid wife was so shaken by the assault that she died within two months. His daughter passed away within a year. Seward moved from the house when he left office in 1869. He died three years later in Auburn, New York.

Subsequent tenants of the building included the YMCA, which was there in the late 1880s. The home's final owner was James G. Blaine, the secretary of state to two presidents. He died there in 1893.

Several of the house's residents during its last two decades heard sounds similar to those experienced by Seward. As time went along, the spirit seemed to be more agitated and the disturbances became more pronounced. At first, Key was blamed for all the paranormal activity, but after Seward's death in Auburn, New York, in 1972, some folks began to suggest the ruckus could be coming from the sometimes hot-tempered former secretary of state. Allegedly, the spectres of Clay and Calhoun also made appearances.

In 1895, the structure was razed to make way for the Lafayette Square Opera House. That theater, too, was demolished, and the US Court of Federal Claims now stands in its place. No ghosts were said to wander the opera house, nor have any been reported in the corridors of the current building—yet.

Chapter 12

The Tolling of the Bell

ST. JOHN'S CHURCH
1525 H Street NW

Hauntings often occur on a particular date, such as the anniversary of an important event in the past, but the phantoms at St. John's Church show up when something new of significance happens in the land of the living. There's also the unpredictable appearance of a phantom organist.

St. John's Church, an Episcopal house of God, dates back almost as far as Washington, DC, itself. The parish was organized in 1815 to serve those living on the west side of the city in the environs of Capitol Hill and the White House. Its chapel is located on the north side of H Street directly across from Lafayette Square, which at the time of its construction was variously known as President's Park, President's Square, and Federal Square.

The sanctuary was designed by Benjamin Henry Latrobe, who was also responsible for the adjacent Decatur House. The church has been altered since, but the original structure was built in the classical shape of a Greek cross, with arms of equal length. Latrobe was creating a church-as-meetinghouse, so the interior was plain, and the pulpit was centrally located with no pillars to obstruct the worshippers' view.

The first services were held at St. John's Church in 1816, making it the oldest (or possibly second oldest) extant building on Lafayette Square. James Madison was president when the house of prayer first opened its doors, and he became a regular congregant. In part due to the president's presence, the church's congregation grew swiftly. It soon included numerous politicians, military leaders, and members of society.

(Dolley Madison, raised Quaker, became a member in 1842, five years after she returned to Washington to live at the Cutts-Madison House. The sanctuary welcomed others in the Madison clan as well, including some Paynes from the maternal side of Dolley's family.)

Within four years of the church's completion, it became necessary to enlarge it. In 1820, the western transept was extended, changing the chapel to the more traditional layout of a Latin cross. At the same time, a Roman Doric portico was added to the main entrance. Later the steeple was modified to have three tiers. Today, much of the exterior of the stucco-covered brick church is painted yellow.

When he attended services, President Madison chose to sit in Pew 54, and he paid an annual rent for it, as was customary for parishioners at the time. Ever since, that bench has been known as the Presidents' Pew. The next five men to follow Madison in office—Monroe, Adams, Jackson, Van Buren, and Harrison—also became members of the church and worshipped in the same pew. Every president since then has attended a service at St. John's at one time or another. Franklin D. Roosevelt took time to pray there on two of his inauguration days. The chapel lives up to its nickname, "The Church of Presidents."

The sanctuary contains twenty-three impressive stained-glass windows, including a unique depiction of the Last Supper over the main altar. Created by Lorin Stained Glass

Windows of Chartres, France, the panes depict the life of Christ but also concentrate on the ministry of St. John, the apostle for whom the church is named. The windows were commissioned in 1883 and installed over the next two years.

Other church treasures include a silver chalice and a gold communion chalice encrusted in jewels. There's also an eighteenth-century prayer book in the Presidents' Pew that's been signed by many of the commanders-in-chief. The pews themselves are the original hardwood benches that have been there for two hundred years.

The chapel's adjoining Parish House originally was home to the British legation to the United States, and it was there that Secretary of State Daniel Webster and Lord Alexander Baring Ashburton signed the treaty that set the disputed border between the New England states and the Canadian Maritime Provinces.

The feature of St. John's Church that's most important to our ghost story is the steeple bell.

The monumental bell, which weighs almost a thousand pounds, was cast by Joseph Warren Revere, son of Paul Revere, at his Boston foundry in August 1822. It was installed at St. John's three months later, on November 30th. (It's one of two Revere bells in the nation's capital but the only one that's been in continuous use.)

The bell was paid for, in part, by a $100 grant in federal funds authorized by President James Monroe. This wasn't a breach of the constitutional separation of church and state: The federal government has full authority over the District of Columbia, including providing for its safety. In addition to being used as a call for worship, the bell could function as an alarm signal in the event of neighborhood emergencies.

Which brings us to our ghosts.

Legend has it that whenever the bell is tolled to mark the death of a notable American, the spectres of six unknown men, dressed in white robes or ceremonial gowns, appear in the Presidents' Pew. They materialize at the stroke of midnight, arms folded and staring straight forward in a show of respect. Moments later, they fade into nothingness.

Some paranormal researchers suggest that the ghosts must have been important Washingtonians, but their theory can't be proved until the revenants are recognized. Interestintly, church records show that a committee was formed no later than 1816 to serve the president whenever he was in the chapel. Could the spectral sextet be somehow connected to that select group?

There have also been a few reports of an ethereal organist showing up at the instrument's keyboard from time to time, but no music is ever heard. The phantom musician's identity is as much a mystery as those of the other six apparitions. And likely to remain so.

Part Four

GEORGETOWN

Situated as far upriver on the Potomac as boats could safely navigate, Georgetown was a thriving Maryland port for forty years before it became part of the nation's capital. It took a separate act of Congress in 1895 to repeal Georgetown's last remaining local laws and to change its street names to mirror those in the rest of the district.

For paranormal enthusiasts, Georgetown has much more to offer than the staircase seen in *The Exorcist*—though no self-guided ghost tour is complete without climbing the steps. The historic enclave is home to more than 250 years of spooks, and they're dying to meet anyone brave enough to seek them out. Care to take a stroll?

Chapter 13
The Halcyon Hauntings

HALCYON HOUSE
3400 Prospect Street NW

The word "halcyon" means peaceful, quiet, serene. But legend has it the spirits haunting Halcyon House are anything but. Their playful pranks—from sorrowful sobbing to making folks float in the air— have been impossible to ignore.

In 1787, Benjamin Stoddert, selected by President John Adams to be the first secretary of the US Navy, built a 30,000-square-foot Federal-style residence in Georgetown overlooking the Potomac River. Stoddert chose Pierre Charles L'Enfant to design its gardens. Stoddert named his home for the Halcyon, a mythical bird whose presence could calm the ocean.

The fable had a deep resonance for Stoddert. He had formed a tobacco export business with two partners in 1783, and shipping his product safely depended on tranquil seas. Halcyon House was a perfect retreat for Stoddert: From the third floor, he could watch his ships enter and leave port.

During the American Revolution, Stoddert had been a cavalry officer, and he became a personal friend of George Washington. In fact, it's claimed that the future president asked Stoddert's help in buying up parcels of land before the District of Columbia's location was announced so the tracts could later be sold to the federal government at a reasonable price.

Stoddert was a prosperous merchant, well positioned in the city's political life, so it was natural that Halcyon House became a popular meeting place for early Washington society. Even famed hostess and future first lady Dolley Madison danced at several parties there.

Stoddert left the Department of the Navy at the end of the Adams's administration. Unfortunately, by then he had neglected his shipping interests to the point that his finances were in shambles. He died almost penniless twelve years later, in 1813.

In 1802, after his wife's death, Stoddert had deeded Halcyon House to his daughter, Elizabeth, and her husband, Thomas Ewell, and the couple stayed there until 1818. A succession of families then lived in the premises over the next half-century. In the years leading up to and during the Civil War, the house was purportedly a station on the Underground Railroad.

John L. Kidwell, a prosperous pharmacist, bought Halcyon House in 1859. Years after the War Between the States, he called in a mason to wall up the entrance to a tunnel in the basement to prevent rat infestation. While the craftsman worked, he heard faint noises that seemed to be moans and crying coming from inside the empty passageway. As he completed his task and set the last piece of plaster in place, a loud scream came from behind the wall, followed by a series of sobs. And even though the shaft was completely closed off, a gust of wind coming from the direction of the wall suddenly blew out Kidwell's carpenter's lamp, leaving him in pitch darkness.

In 1900, the property was bought by Albert Adsit Clemons. It's often purported that he was a nephew of Mark Twain, whose real name was Samuel Clemens, but there are no records confirming the relationship. Clemons also spelled his name differently.

Clemons had a bizarre belief: He thought that by continually making changes to his house, it was possible for him to ward off death. He connected the coach house to the main building and added ten apartments to the north face and the sides of the structure. But some of his other architectural alterations were downright bizarre.

Clemons added hallways inside the house but then walled them off, built small rooms within larger rooms, and placed a tiny crypt in one chamber. In a March 1943 newspaper article, Dorothy W. Sterling (wife of the US ambassador to Sweden and one of the later owners of Halcyon House) described some of Clemons's weird renovations: "There are dozens of tiny rooms—some of them hardly large enough for a table or chair. There are staircases that lead nowhere, doors that open on blank walls, and closets that open on other closets."

(This incessant remodeling was very similar to that done in California at the end of the nineteenth century by Sarah Winchester, heiress to the Winchester repeating rifle fortune. At a séance in 1884, a medium told Sarah that she had to leave her home in New Haven, Connecticut, move to the West Coast, and build a new house. The seer insisted that Sarah's recently deceased husband and baby had been killed by angry spirits—innocent victims of the Winchester rifle—and if Sarah ever stopped adding onto her new home, the phantoms would come for her as well. Sarah purchased a mansion already under construction in San Jose, California, and, to trick the ghosts, incorporated dozens of architectural oddities such as dead-end staircases and a door on the second floor that opened out onto the open air. She went so far as to plant a double row of giant palm trees on both sides of the driveway leading up to her house so she could hide between them, looking for apparitions. The Winchester House can now be visited as a tourist attraction, and some say it really is haunted—by Sarah Winchester herself!)

According to legend, Clemons's constant tinkering with Halcyon House awakened the ghost of Benjamin Stoddert, who began to revisit his old home. Most times the phantom, dressed in tan, would be seen in a south drawing room, sitting in what had been Stoddert's favorite chair when he was alive. Other times the apparition would walk through the house, frequently whispering but too quietly to be understood. Stoddert's spectre has also been seen at one of the dormer windows facing the Potomac, with one eye at a spyglass surveying his long-gone ships on the river.

Clemons was an eccentric landlord as well. He advertised "Apartments for Rent; No Children; No Dogs; No Electricity." That's right: he wouldn't install electricity, Still, he somehow managed to find people willing to lease the rooms. Then, every year he made all of the occupants switch apartments, claiming it was necessary to equalize the strain on the building's foundation.

In perhaps a final peculiarity, Clemons placed a clause in his last will and testament instructing the attending physician at the time of his death to "pierce or puncture my heart sufficiently for the purpose of absolute certainty of death." Clemons died on March 17, 1938, but it's doubtful his morbid directive was ever carried out. Perhaps if it had been, he wouldn't have returned from the dead.

Over the next fifty years, there were reports that several photographs and artwork mysteriously dropped off the walls. On one occasion, a mirror that was hanging over the fireplace fell during the night, splintering the mantelpiece. The debris was discovered the next day neatly piled in a corner. The mirror itself was unbroken, but there was a large, indelible "X" written on it.

Ashtrays would fill up with water, and windows would open on their own. Doors would open and close by themselves. Lights turned themselves on and off—for a time, every Thursday between 1 a.m. and 2 a.m. Groans and crying were heard throughout the house, especially the basement, and other strange sounds emanated from the attic. Some paranormalists suggest that the mournful sounds may have come from the wraiths of slaves who, weak and sick from their escape and flight northward, died while hiding in Halcyon House.

Perhaps most ominous of all, a dark, brooding, human form was sometimes spotted climbing the main staircase. So far its identity is uncertain, but many believe that the dark shade was Clemons. A different ghost, an aged female phantom, was seen rocking in a chair in the guest bedroom.

One of the most frequently told ghost stories of Halcyon House involves a visit by two friends of one of the owners after Clemons's death. The guests, a husband and wife, stayed overnight in the master bedroom. They awoke the next morning to find themselves hovering a foot in the air above the bed. As a further surprise, their bodies had somehow revolved in the middle of the night so that their heads were at the bottom of the bed. Between 1963 and 1972 there were three such instances of levitation occurring to people who slept in that second-floor bedroom.

A tale surfaced in the 1970s about the six-year-old grandson of another Halcyon owner. The boy came down to breakfast one morning and told his grandparents that an elderly woman he didn't know had visited his room the night before to tuck him into bed. She whispered that she wouldn't be back but not to tell anyone. It seems to have been a one-time haunting, because no one else has ever seen the ghost of the little old lady.

Architect Edmund Dreyfuss purchased the house in 1966 and hoped to develop it into a commercial property. His plans didn't pan out, and in 1978, his son, John, an artist and sculptor, took over Halcyon House and began a seventeen-year renovation. His makeover included the removal of all of Clemons's unorthodox additions and the partial restoration of the house to its nineteenth-century appearance. Dreyfuss turned the ground level into his studio, and some of the rooms upstairs were made into living quarters. Other areas became rental facilities for parties and special events. It was during this period, in 1971, that Halcyon House was listed on the National Register of Historic Places.

In 2012, Dr. Sachiko Kuno and Dr. Ryuki Ueno bought the property for an estimated eleven million dollars. Today, it's one of two headquarters for their S&R Foundation.

Paranormal activity seems to have stopped at Halcyon House. But is it gone for good? It may be too soon to tell. Eternity's a very long time.

Chapter 14
Cheaper
by the Dozen

OLD STONE HOUSE MUSEUM
3051 M STREET NW

Ghosts tend to haunt places, not people, so the longer a house sticks around, the greater the odds are that some of its former residents will return from the Other Side to visit. One of the oldest buildings in DC is harboring at least a dozen spirits.

In 1764, years before the District of Columbia came into being, a young couple named Christopher and Rachel Layman moved with their two sons from Philadelphia to the growing port of Georgetown. They could not have conceived that two and a half centuries later, their humble home would become part of the nation's folklore—and ghostlore.

Georgetown, located in the Province of Maryland, was only thirteen years old when Layman bought Lot Three, a property facing Bridge Street (now M Street NW), for one pound ten shillings. The Layman house had one story and was built of blue fieldstone, quarried about two miles up the Potomac River. The stone walls were about two to three feet thick, the floors were packed dirt, and the ceiling with its solid oak beams was low to conserve heat. The family's few possessions included Christopher's tools, a Bible, some furniture, and a stove. In addition, out back they planted fruit trees, an herb and vegetable garden, and a bit of tobacco. They also kept cows, chicken, and hogs.

The family lived there for about three years. After Christopher's sudden death, Rachael remarried in 1767. She sold the house to Mrs. Cassandra Chew, an upper-middle-class widow who already owned several other properties in and around Georgetown. Chew made several major additions to the Layman house, including a rear kitchen and, by 1775, a second and third floor. When Mrs. Chew died in 1807, she willed the house to Mary Smith Brumley, her oldest daughter, who was also well-to-do.

Over time, the histories of Old Stone House and the nearby Suter's Tavern (also known as Fountain Inn) became inextricably intertwined. One legend says that George Washington and Pierre Charles L'Enfant used the Old Stone House as their headquarters while planning the layout of Washington, DC.

What actually happened is this: In 1791, when Washington, L'Enfant, and Thomas Jefferson traveled to the new capital, they stayed at Suter's Tavern, which was owned by John Suter. While there, Washington met with many of the local landowners. Maryland had agreed to cede property to the district, but it was still in private hands and had to be purchased by the federal government.

Around 1810, Mary Brumley rented the front room of Old Stone House (today, the museum bookstore) to Suter's namesake son, a clockmaker, to use as his shop. (Subsequent owners would also lease out the front room to local merchants.) Upon his father's death, John Suter Jr. inherited the hostelry. The inn was probably located at what is now 31st and K Streets NW.

(There may have been another connection between the Brumleys and the Suters as well, although it's mostly conjecture. Two of Mary Smith Brumley's daughters were named Sarah Maria Suter and Ann Suter, suggesting that at some point the families intermarried.)

Records are incomplete but it's known that, after the Brumleys, several other tenants and businesses either owned, lived in, or operated out of the Old Stone House. Its upstairs was sometimes rented out to travelers, and rumor has it that it housed a bordello in the 1930s. In the early 1950s, Parkway Motor Company, a used-car dealership, had their offices there, and the rear garden was paved over as a parking lot.

Old Stone House came under the protection of the National Park Service in 1953. Convinced by local residents that the building had great historical value as the last remaining Georgetown structure on its original foundation, the federal government bought it for $90,000.

The NPS set to work restoring the house and refurnishing it to its pre-1800 appearance. Many pieces were donated by Georgetown residents. The Park Service also bought and put on display a grandfather clock that had been built in the house by John Suter Jr.

Old Stone House and Museum was opened to the public for tourism in 1960. Though the site is under the umbrella of the National Park Service, it's administered on a day-to-day basis as part of Rock Creek Park.

The house is one of the most haunted places in Washington, DC. With the exception of the apparition that may be the original owner, Christopher Layman, all of the ghosts remain unidentified.

Ladies first.

The translucent figure of a woman has been seen cooking in the kitchen. She may or may not be the same spectre that materializes near the fireplace wearing a brown dress dating to the 1700s. A large woman—not obese but thickset—also shows up in the kitchen or on the staircase leading to the second floor. She always wears a Civil War–era gown. Another female phantom with ringlets in her hair (sometimes described as a girl, other times a young woman) runs up and down those same steps. Up on the third floor, the ghost of a woman appears in a rocking chair.

And then there are the male spirits—lots of them. One spectre seems to be a craftsman and has been described in ghost literature as "Germanic." A man in Federal-era breeches and long stockings is often seen in the kitchen; another with long, dark blond hair and wearing a blue jacket has been spied through a window in the front room. A fourth phantom, dressed in Colonial garb, shows up in the master bedroom on the second floor.

There are also two boys on the roster of wraiths. A small Caucasian lad that staff has called Joey runs from one end of the third floor to the other. A young African-American boy is seen in that same hallway and other parts of the house. The latter boy may have been one of the slaves who worked there before the War Between the States. Almost certainly, slaves tended Layman's garden and livestock. Tax records from 1800 show that Mrs. Chew owned six slaves, and Mrs. Brumley had fifteen slaves in 1826. (One of them, Tabitha, later purchased freedom for herself and a child for two hundred and one dollars.)

The sound of children's disembodied laughter has been reported in the house, and at least one object was seen moving on its own: A rolling pin fell off the kitchen cupboard, neatly missing the china, and wound up on the floor in the middle of the room.

The Old Stone House has one more apparition—its most active—and somewhere along the way it acquired the name George. His presence has been felt throughout the building, but he mainly haunts the third floor bedroom. George is one of Washington's few malevolent ghosts, and he seems to dislike females in particular. Women have reported being pushed, choked, knifed, and sexually assaulted by the invisible spirit. Folks often know when George is around because they feel an inexplicable cold spot or are overcome with a sudden, deep-set fear or anxiety.

You're no doubt safe if you visit Old Stone House Museum, but be on the lookout. With a dozen or so ghosts on the loose, you never know what might happen.

Chapter 15

Good Housekeeping

FOXALL HOUSE
3123 DUMBARTON STREET NW

It's nice to have a housekeeper on the job. But when she continues to report for duty long after crossing over to the Next World, the "help" can become a "horror."

Born in Monmouth, England, on May 24, 1758, Henry Foxall entered the iron industry in Britain and Ireland. In 1797, he moved to Philadelphia where he and Robert Morris Jr., established the Eagle Iron Works along the Schuylkill River. Two years later, the firm received a commission from Benjamin Stoddert, secretary of the Navy, to produce cannon for the federal government.

In 1800, Foxall ended his partnership with Morris, moved to Georgetown, and started his own company, the Columbian Ordinance Foundry (also seen as the Foxall or Columbia Foundry). Located on the Potomac River, the iron works produced cannon shot and gun carriages in addition to the cannons themselves. His munitions were vital in the US Navy's fight against the Barbary Pirates in North Africa and in engagements with the British during the War of 1812.

Foxall's plant also provided cast iron for the Capitol Building as well as iron pieces such as clock weights, window sashes, fireplace backs, and stoves for Mulberry Row at Monticello, Thomas Jefferson's 5,000-acre plantation.

The manufacturer was a personal friend of the president, whom he had met back in Philadelphia before the US government moved to Washington. In fact, Foxall may have made the move to DC at Jefferson's request. The chief executive, who served from 1801 to 1809, was known to visit Foxall's Georgetown home, where the two played duets on the violin.

In addition to operating his own foundry, in 1809 Foxall helped Virginia set up an iron works in Richmond to supply the state's militia with cannon. Foxall also was involved in shipping, real estate, and banking. After retiring in 1815, Foxall returned to England, where he remarried. (His first wife had died some years earlier.) He came back to Georgetown and served as mayor from 1821 to 1823. Soon after leaving office, Foxall sailed to England once again, where he died after a brief illness on December 11, 1823.

Foxall's main residence in Georgetown was located where 34th Street NW met the C&O Canal, sitting on the southeast corner. He also maintained a "summer" or "country" house on a farm just outside Georgetown near modern-day Foxhall Road. Neither home is standing today.

Henry Foxall also had a third house on Dumbarton Street. Until recently it was believed that he built it in 1800, used it as his own home, and then deeded it to his daughter, Mary Ann, and her husband, Samuel McKinney, a merchant, when they married in 1813. Foxall bought the land in 1812, but he may not have moved into the house right away. Research shows there are no tax records for the "new building on Dumbarton Street" until 1819.

The architecture of the three-story structure (plus basement and attic) is primarily Classical Revival with a few characteristics from the late Federal period. Interior rooms are as high as fourteen feet, and the gabled roof outside is covered with slate. The house stayed in the Foxall-McKinney family until 1944. Kenyon Bolton, who owned the home from 1946 to 1956, is credited with restoring it. He also hired Rose Freely, who was an important Washington landscape artist, to design its gardens.

The house on Dumbarton was still owned by descendants of Henry Foxall in the 1890s when the ghost of an elderly female housekeeper began to appear in the hallway on the third floor. Newspapers at the time described the spectre as "a diaphanous aged woman." She would usually materialize just before 10 p.m., and whenever she showed up all of the lights in the house would go out. That included any type of lighting: electric, gas lamp, or candle flame.

It's unknown who first saw the spirit, but by the turn of the twentieth century her presence was well known to local residents. They called the phenomenon the "ten-o'clock ritual." It's believed the apparition was a longtime servant of the Foxalls whose name has been lost to time, but her image can be seen in an old family daguerreotype. The bedrooms for the Foxall children were on the third floor, and the housekeeper rigidly enforced "lights out" at ten. Legend has it that she returned from the Other Side so she could continue imposing the rule.

The ghost never caused any trouble—other than that annoying tendency to turn out the lights. And she never interacted with any of the living. Reports of new sightings died off in the early 1950s, but that doesn't mean phenomena in the house stopped.

While doing additional research for the 1998 update of his classic book about Washington ghosts, author John Alexander met a woman who had lived in Foxall from the

1950s (when she was a teenager) until the 1970s. She confessed that the entire family had experienced paranormal activity during their time in the house, but they had chosen not to talk about it.

She and her brother would sometimes hear disembodied footsteps walking up and down the staircase. Her brother was once alone, talking on the phone in the study off the foyer, when he heard the distinctive sound of the house's large, wooden front door open and close. He then heard someone walking in the hall, so he put down the handset to go see who had come in. There was no one there.

Another time the entire family was watching TV together when reception went out. This was before remote controls existed, so the father got up to check the on-off switch. He discovered that the button had somehow been turned off without anyone touching it. On another occasion, everyone came down to breakfast to find a favorite painting had raised itself off the wall mounting and was lying on the kitchen table. While on vacation, their house sitter called to say she had just seen a ghost in one of the hallways and wanted to know whether it had a name.

Finally, in the 1970s, the family's then-housekeeper encountered a spectre while the children were off at college. The apparition said she was there to collect her things and was leaving. Apparently, the Foxall phantom has not been seen since.

There may have been another ghost in the house as well. On very rare occasions, residents on the second floor heard the sound of the dining room furniture being moved around on the first floor, but when they investigated, nothing was ever disturbed. Folklore says that one of the male owners of Foxall House hid his love letters under the dining room floorboards and that workmen found them years after the man died. Is it his ghost fruitlessly searching for the lost missives that caused the noises coming from the dining room? Perhaps we'll never know.

Chapter 16
The Bridge Street Crossing

M STREET BRIDGE
M Street NW

K STREET BRIDGE
K Street NW

Phantoms from the past often continue to walk a city's streets years after they've Crossed Over, and in the case of the District of Columbia, this phenomenon also includes ghosts visiting two of the capital's many bridges.

Long before Europeans reached America's shores, the indigenous people fished in Rock Creek, used its stones to make tools, and hunted on its shores. By the beginning of the seventeenth century, English explorers of the New World had claimed the land for their mother country, despite its being populated by Native Americans.

Georgetown was founded in 1751 at the uppermost point that ocean vessels could sail up the Potomac. It also happened to be where Rock Creek met the river.

During the town's colonial years and into the early 1800s, farmers grew tobacco in the Rock Creek area, but by the mid-nineteenth century, the crop had exhausted the soil. Shifting to wheat and corn gave the land a second agricultural life, and several mills (most notably Peirce Mill) were built along Rock Creek to grind the local grain into flour.

In 1788, two years before the District of Columbia was established, a wooden bridge was built over Rock Creek at the eastern edge of Georgetown. The road over the bridge was, naturally enough, called Bridge Street.

A sturdier overpass, also made of wood, was constructed in 1802 (some sources say 1800). It was a drawbridge because Rock Creek was still navigable. By the time a replacement was required in 1839, the need for a draw-bridge was gone: the creek had silted up, and a quay on the Potomac blocked the mouth of the river. A wooden covered bridge was erected in place of the old drawbridge.

During the Civil War, most of the trees in the Rock Creek area were cut down to create barricades and other defensive structures to prevent Confederate armies from entering the capital. Also, several Union forts were constructed around DC, including Fort Stevens. (President Abraham Lincoln was present in the fort to observe the Union victory over an assault by General Jubal A. Early's Confederate troops in July 1864.)

A steel-truss bridge was put up in the covered bridge's place in 1871. Then, in 1890, Congress set aside roughly 2,000 acres in the northwest corner of Washington, DC, to create Rock Creek Park, a federally managed urban woodland.

In 1895, Congress passed a law that repealed George-town's remaining local ordinances and required the commu-nity to change all of its street names to conform to the rest of the District. Thus, Bridge Street became an extension of M Street NW.

In 1925, the steel bridge over Rock Creek was closed when it was judged to be unsafe. The current M Street

Bridge was constructed from 1929 to 1930. It spans both the creek and a new, major roadway alongside it known as the Rock Creek and Potomac Parkway (or simply Rock Creek Parkway).

In 1933, Rock Creek Park became part of the US National Park System. Today it's tasked with administering several other landmarks under the park system, including the haunted Old Stone Inn in Georgetown—which seems appropriate since the M Street Bridge appears to be haunted as well.

The bridge's first ghost story dates to early post-Revolutionary times. The apparition is a drummer boy from Falls Church, Virginia, who drowned in Rock Creek after he was blown off the original bridge by a strong gust of wind. For many years after his death, people could hear his drumming on quiet evenings—soft at first and then growing louder as the invisible spectre neared the center of the bridge. The sound then suddenly stopped, presumably when the boy's spirit had reached the spot where he fell to his death.

There are many variations to the saga of the young drummer. Some say the youngster's death actually took place during the War of 1812. As British troops raced toward the capital on the night of August 24, 1814, American militiamen fled the city, hoping to regroup and fight another day. The boy took up a post on the rocks at the Little Falls crossing of the Potomac River, beating his drum non-stop to guide the retreating soldiers to safety. He stayed in position throughout the gale that followed the Burning of Washington, but at some point he was swept away by the swollen river. Ever since, people have heard the steady beat of the boy's drum on nights when there are summer storms. Yet another version of the story circulating in the mid-nineteenth century claimed the drummer had been murdered in a house in Georgetown. His invisible spirit returned to haunt the residence by beating his also-unseen drumsticks on one of the mansion's mahogany tables.

Legend has it that the original bridge over Rock Creek collapsed during a severe rainstorm, taking with it a stagecoach, its driver, and horses. Afterward it was said that on dark, moonless nights, a phantom stagecoach could be seen in Georgetown silently barreling toward the overpass. Halfway across the M Street Bridge, it simply disappeared, often accompanied by a clap of thunder and a flash of lightning. Regular reports of this haunting and that of the drummer boy lessened over the years, but the sightings have never completely stopped.

There's supposedly a spirit that haunts the K Street Bridge over Rock Creek, too. The phantom is a headless man who's been seen both on the bridge and on nearby Georgetown streets. There's been conjecture that the wraith was a victim during the Civil War or that he was beheaded by a mob after committing some heinous crime. Nothing is known for certain about the sinister shade, including his identity or why he chose to haunt the bridge. Stories about the ghost began in the early nineteenth century, so he would have to date from the time of the stone arch built on the site in 1792 or the wooden bridge that replaced it in 1869. The apparition is seldom seen today, but he may still be around.

Back in the 1800s, there were also reports of a headless horseman, who may or may not be the same ghost haunting the K Street Bridge. He would gallop on his steed just south of Georgetown on a narrow strip of land between the Potomac River and the old Chesapeake and Ohio Canal.

Rock Creek Park is popular with nature-lovers, joggers, and even motorists seeking a pleasant drive close to downtown. For more than two hundred years, the bridges over Rock Creek have been a vital link between Georgetown and central Washington. They've also been two of the best places to spot some of DC's legendary spooks.

Chapter 17

The Echoes of War

GEORGETOWN BLUFFS ON THE POTOMAC RIVER
14TH STREET BRIDGE RIVERBANK

"Tramp, tramp, tramp, the boys are marching . . . " Start with some British and colonial soldiers, throw in a few French troops and Indian warriors, stir in a dash of deception during the War Between the States, and you have the recipe for a recurring ghost story in Georgetown.

Captain John Smith—yes, the Pocahontas guy—was one of the first Europeans to sail up the Potomac River on a voyage of discovery. From June 2 to July 21, 1608, he and a crew of fourteen sailed up the river as part of an attempt to find the fabled passageway to the Orient.

Smith's navigation of the Potomac took him as far as Little Falls, about a mile upriver from the present-day District of Columbia. Along the way, the Englishmen met with several Native American tribes. A Wicocomoco man named Mosco joined Smith's party and acted as a guide for much of the journey. (Mosco had a heavy beard, an unusual trait for a Native American, which suggested he had a bit of European ancestry.)

Smith's diaries didn't go into great detail about his days on the Potomac, but his descriptions of the forests and abundant game were enough to pique the interest of his fellow countrymen. In 1632, English fur trader Henry Fleet established a post in the Nacotchtank village of Tohoga, which was situated as far up the river as boats could safely navigate. A century later, in 1751, Georgetown would be founded on the site.

Presumably the town was named for George II, who was the king of England, but the municipality might have taken its name from George Gordon or George Beall, who collectively owned much of the property that became Georgetown.

By the time the town was officially established, it was already a busy warehouse and trading center. It remained an independent community until it became part of Washington, DC.

In pre-Revolutionary days, the biggest thorn in the side of the British was the French, whose explorers had claimed much of the Mississippi basin, the Great Lakes, eastern Canada, and several islands in the Caribbean.

And, of course, there were always the Indians. Caught between two great European superpowers encroaching on their lands, they made alliances with one side or the other, depending upon which one they thought could benefit them most.

The basis for one of Georgetown's most famous ghost stories dates to this period, specifically to 1758. The country at that time was in the middle of the French and Indian War, which took place from 1754 to 1763. The hostilities in America were over which country would control the lucrative fur trade and be the dominant force in the continent's interior.

The conflict was the fourth in a series of battles between England and France. The first three began in Europe and spread to the colonies. The fourth started in

America and made its way to Europe and was known there as the Seven Years' War. In North America, the armies were primarily made up of colonists, reinforced by soldiers from their respective home countries as well as whatever native tribes they could convince to join them. Thus, the name "French and Indian War" refers to the two main parties who fought the British.

By the middle of the eighteenth century, the confluence of the Allegheny, Monongahela, and Ohio Rivers in western Pennsylvania (today the site of Pittsburgh) had acquired strategic importance—for trade, for protection of local settlers, and as a route westward for pioneers. Beginning in the early 1750s, the French started constructing fortifications from Lake Erie southward. In 1753, concerned about the encroachment on what they considered to be British territory, the Virginia Colony sent a twenty-one-year-old envoy named George Washington to one of the strongholds, Fort LeBoeuf. Washington advised the French to leave the region if they wished to avoid military conflict, but he was sent off packing.

The Virginian lieutenant governor, Robert Dinwiddle, quickly dispatched a small company to construct Fort Prince George at the Allegheny-Monongahela convergence to prevent the French from building there. Work began in February 1754. Two months later, five hundred French and Canadian soldiers showed up and easily forced the British to surrender. The French tore down the garrison and built Fort Duquesne in its place.

In May 1754, troops under George Washington engaged the French at the Battle of Jumonville Glen, resulting in an uneasy truce. On April 14, 1755, six colonial governors had a meeting with General Edward Braddock, the newly installed commander in chief of the British colonies. They convinced the general that a major offensive was necessary to remove the French. It was decided that the British would attack four different French forts simultaneously. Braddock would personally lead the assault on Fort Duquesne.

It took two months to prepare for the battle. By late June, General Braddock had assembled 1,300 soldiers in Georgetown for the long march to western Pennsylvania. The troops collected on Observation Hill and on the banks of the Potomac River, close to where Long Bridge, a wooden toll bridge, would be built in 1809.

(Long Bridge would be the second bridge to cross the Potomac in Washington, DC. A bridge had been built at Little Falls near the site of today's Chain Bridge in 1797.)

Braddock and his men never made it to Fort Duquesne. The general wasn't happy about having to use Native Americans as guides, so he only took eight Mingo scouts with him. As a result, he had insufficient warning that an army of about eight hundred French and Canadian soldiers, along with their Ottawa and Potawatomi allies, had left the fort in an attempt to ambush him.

Also, Braddock underestimated the difficulty in transporting his artillery over the frontier roads. As he neared Fort Duquesne, he split his army in two and sent the faster column of soldiers ahead, commanded by Lieutenant Colonel Thomas Gage.

The French and Indians met the British troops at present-day Braddock, Pennsylvania, about ten miles east of Pittsburgh. Braddock soon caught up with his cannon and supply wagons, but by then the British were on the defensive. The local Indians had the advantage of knowing the terrain, plus the cannon wasn't particularly effective in a forested area.

Still, the British held their own until General Braddock was mortally wounded. His forces retreated, but the Native Americans descended upon them as they reached the Monongahela River. Colonel Washington managed to set up a rear defensive guard, allowing the remaining British to escape, and the French and Indians chose not to pursue.

Approximately 450 of Braddock's men were killed in the Battle of the Monongahela; another 400 or more were wounded. General Braddock died four days later during the trek back to Virginia, and Washington oversaw his burial on the road near Fort Necessity.

The French held onto Fort Duquesne for the duration of the French and Indian War. But in the end, the British were victorious. Most of the fighting in the American colonies was finished by 1760, but the Seven Years' War dragged on in Europe for another three years. The Treaty of Paris, which ended the North American conflict, was finally signed in February 1763.

The Battle of the Monongahela is long over, but the massacre has had paranormal repercussions. By the time of the Civil War, a legend was well established that each year on the anniversary of Braddock's departure for Pennsylvania, people standing on the Georgetown bluffs and at the spot along the river where the troops had assembled hear the disembodied sounds of horse hooves, rumbling wheels of artillery wagons, rattling swords, tromping boots, and the muffled shouts of long-dead officers. The noises are so distinct that during the War Between the States, a party of Union soldiers at Long Bridge mistook them for an approaching Confederate army.

Long Bridge has been rebuilt many times over the decades. Today it's a railroad bridge, part of five structures collectively known as the 14th Street Bridge. Many of the historic homes on the ridge overlooking the Potomac have given way to modern buildings. Nonetheless, the haunting sounds of the doomed army's departure echoes through the aether in Georgetown, even after two hundred fifty years.

Chapter 18

The Maidens' Curse

THREE SISTERS ROCKS
POTOMAC RIVER JUST NORTH OF KEY BRIDGE

To the casual observer, they simply look like stony outgrowths, poking their heads above the surface of the river. But to others, the Three Sisters Rocks hold a deep secret that dates back half a millennium: a curse that's striking down disbelievers to this very day.

Three small islands, little more than granite rocks, jut out of the Potomac River north of the Francis Scott Key Bridge about a mile or so south of the Chain Bridge. It's claimed that dozens of people have died trying to cross the river there or even sail close to the boulders because of an ancient Native American curse.

Prior to European colonization, the area was populated by a patchwork of individual tribes and loose alliances. The legend of the Three Sisters Rocks dates back to before the Jamestown settlement in 1607, and it comes down to us from the Powhatan Confederacy. Their Algonquian-speaking tribes occupied the lands along the Potomac River, especially the west bank. (The river itself is named for the Confederacy's Patawomeck tribe.)

Rival tribes in the region, especially the Susquehannock to the east, often engaged the Powhatan in battle, seeking to control trade along the river, the fertile fields, and the forests filled with plentiful game. The Three Sisters myth concerns one particular engagement in which the Susquehannock set up a long siege and were almost successful in decimating the Powhatan on the Virginia side of the river. The Powhatan were able to drive their adversaries back across the Potomac, and, once the coast was clear, they crossed the river in search of much-needed provisions. The Powhatan chief insisted that his three sons stay behind, because he thought they were too young for battle if the hunting party chanced upon the enemy.

The prideful boys would not take no for an answer. Once the village warriors were out of sight, the young men put a risky plan into action. They would take the tribe's one remaining canoe and bring back fish for the women, children, and old men until their fellow tribesmen could return with more food. Their bravery, they felt, would win their father's honor and respect.

The best fishing was close to the far shore, however, and the boys didn't know that the Susquehannock had left a small scouting party behind. The battle-hardened fighters easily overpowered the three young men, who were captured and killed within sight of the remaining Powhatan villagers—including the three daughters of the tribe's shaman.

The girls were in love with the chief's sons, and they were devastated by their deaths. Overcome with grief and hatred, they came up with a scheme for revenge. They would cross the river and walk into the Susquehannock camp. Using the lure of their natural beauty and some of the magical powers learned from their medicine-man father, they would bewitch the chief. He, in turn, would give them as brides to the warriors who had killed the Powhatan chief's sons. Once alone with the murderers, the three sisters would make them suffer slow, painful, torturous deaths.

Without a canoe at hand, the girls lashed several logs together as a raft. Telling no one, they set off from the riverbank. They were midstream before they encountered the strong current of the Potomac, which threatened to topple them or sweep them out to sea. Realizing that, either way, they were doomed, the girls made a pact. If they weren't able to ford the Potomac at that location, they declared, then nobody would be able to—ever—through the end of time. Gathering in a circle, they recited a powerful incantation and cursed the river crossing. Then, sealing the spell with their own deaths, they jumped into the swirling waters.

It's said the skies immediately darkened. Thunder crashed as lightning tore through the clouds, with bolts striking the river. The storm raged overnight, and when it cleared the next morning, three large granite stones were seen sticking out of the river precisely where the girls had perished.

The outcrops' sudden appearance was deemed supernatural, and it gave rise to the belief that the three sisters had transformed themselves into the boulders to stand as sentinels. They would be a constant reminder of their tragic tale, and they would act as a warning for those who were foolhardy enough to try to cross the river there.

In another version of the story, the three Anacostan sisters were daughters of the chief, and they had fallen in love with three Powhatan braves. Because marriages between the two tribes were unthinkable, the girls had to "elope." One dark evening they set out in canoes, heading for the opposite shore, despite a brewing storm. Their tribe's medicine man found out about the plan, went down to the river, and called for them to return. He shouted that if they didn't come back they would surely die. Suddenly, otherworldly lights and spirit voices surrounded their boats and, terrified, the maidens jumped into the rushing waves and drowned. Three great rocks rose from the water to mark the spot where they breathed their last.

Still another variation doesn't mention the Native American connection at all. The victims were simply three sisters paddling a small boat on the river. Their craft drifted into the rocks (which were already there), and the girls tumbled out and drowned. Their doleful, disembodied cries have returned as a death omen. The sounds echo to shore from the three boulders just before the river claims another victim.

Perhaps the river curse is real. Records are inexact, but it's thought that hundreds have died trying to forge the Potomac at that point. According to police, there are still several deaths a year by swimmers, fishermen, or casual boaters who think they can manage the swift-flowing water near the rocks.

Also, although there have been many discussions about building a bridge in the proximity of the islands, no proposal has ever come to fruition. The last attempt to construct a bridge near the Three Sisters Rocks took place in early 1970s. Its framework was already in place when a freakishly wild storm rolled through the capital, collapsing the foundation.

Trips to the islets are allowed, but you'd have to boat over. (Don't even think about trying to swim it!) Each rock measures only 1,000 to 2,000 square feet, and their sizes change depending on the river's water level. There's nothing to see on the Three Sisters Rocks other than some shrubs and small trees—not even a marker telling the Powhatan legend. Is it worth tempting your fate to get to them?

Chapter 19

The Devil's Downfall

THE EXORCIST STEPS
Prospect and 36th Streets NW to M Street NW

PROSPECT HOUSE
3508 Prospect Street NW

GEORGETOWN UNIVERSITY
3700 0 Street NW

GALLAUDET UNIVERSITY
800 Florida Avenue NE

There's more to the paranormal world than ghosts. There are all sorts of other spirits out there, and some of them are not very nice. Take, for example, the story of demon possession in the book and the film The Exorcist.

Seventy-five steep and very narrow steps lead from a high ridge of Georgetown down almost to the river's edge. The Capital Traction Company built them in 1895 next to a red brick building it used to house the trolley cars that were then part of the city's transit system.

The stairs aren't marked. They don't have to be. They already draw a steady stream of tourists and curiosity seekers. The steps stretch between Prospect and 36th Streets at the top of the bluff down to M Street at the bottom. The foot of the stairs is next to a gas station, across the road from Key Bridge. The staircase itself is tucked into a cleft in the hillside and set back from the road, almost hidden from view.

William Peter Blatty introduced the staircase to readers in his 1971 horror novel *The Exorcist*. But the steps truly became embedded in the public's consciousness two years later when they were seen in the breathtaking climax of the film adaptation. The steps are very close to Georgetown University, so they were no doubt familiar to Blatty, who graduated from the school in 1950. (Jogging up and down the stairs is a popular exercise regimen for students and local residents.)

The movie version of *The Exorcist* is framed as a detective's investigation into—spoiler alert!—the unusual death of two Jesuit priests. The story focuses on a twelve-year old girl named Regan, portrayed in the film by Linda Blair, who is living in the Georgetown district of Washington, DC, with her mother, Chris MacNeil, a famous actress, played by Ellen Burstyn. After Regan innocently plays with a Ouija board, strange poltergeist-like phenomena begin to take place in the house.

(Many paranormal experts warn that a Ouija board is not a toy. Its use could accidentally summon unknown, unwanted, and dangerous spirits. The Ouija board isn't the only ghost reference in *The Exorcist*. One of the characters mentions a fraudulent medium who, years earlier, had studied to be a Jesuit priest. The aside is most likely referring to Daniel Dunglas Home, pronounced "Hume," who was the most famous American medium of the nineteenth century—the Spiritualist movement's first superstar.)

Having unwittingly conjured up a malevolent spirit, Regan begins to undergo a change. She has wild mood swings with angry outbursts. Physical manifestations follow, including scratch marks on her body and incontinence. After a battery of grueling doctors' tests and medications failing to cure Regan's inexplicable illness, her mother turns to a local Jesuit priest, Father Damien Karras (portrayed in the movie by Jason Miller). She asks him to perform an exorcism.

Though undergoing a crisis of faith himself, Father Karras agrees to see the girl. He is dumbfounded by Regan's appearance. She has undergone a complete transformation. Words are clawed into her flesh seemingly from the inside; she's able to spin her head a full 360 degrees; she can levitate and produce projectile vomiting at will. Karras concedes that the girl may be possessed by a demon.

The local bishop assigns an aged but experienced exorcist, Father Lankester Merrin (played by Max von Sydow) to assist Karras. The priests perform a series of rites that take their toll on them, both physically and mentally. At one point, Karras briefly steps out of the room. When he returns he finds Merrin dead, presumably of a heart attack. He then realizes that the demon had killed Merrin and challenges the spirit to leave Regan's body. Take possession of him instead, he demands—a much more precious prize than a little girl.

The demon complies, and in a moment of tragic self-sacrifice, Father Karras hurls himself out of the second-story bedroom window. He falls to his death, tumbling down that infamous staircase. Released from the demon's grasp, Regan returns to normal.

The Exorcist was complete fiction, but Blatty based his novel on a real-life exorcism of a Mount Rainier, Maryland, boy that was reported in the *Washington Post* in 1949.

(Other sources say that the child was from nearby Cottage City.) The boy had been plagued by his bed shaking, his desk and books moving at school, the sound of odd scraping noises, and inexplicable scratches appearing on his body forming legible words. His parents took him to St. Louis, where an aunt and uncle lived. Two area Jesuit priests performed an exorcism over the boy, beginning at St. Xavier College Church rectory and finishing their work at Alexian Brother's Hospital. (While doing research for the book, Blatty spoke with Father William F. Bowdern, a Jesuit priest from St. Louis who claimed to have been one of the priests who performed the youngster's exorcism.)

When it came time to film *The Exorcist,* director William Friedkin decided to shoot several scenes on location in Georgetown. The best remembered, of course, is the one at the staircase, but there are also recognizable glimpses of Key Bridge and a bridge over the C&O Canal. Locations on the campus of Georgetown University appear in the movie, too, including the exterior of Healy Hall, the interior of Dahlgren Chapel, and the office of the president of the university (doubling as the Archbishop's office). There's an eerie, atmospheric shot of Burstyn walking down the gloomy, darkened streets of Georgetown as well.

Often when a ghost or horror film is released, its publicist spreads rumors that strange things occurred while it was being shot. But several people associated with *The Exorcist* swear the movie really was cursed. A studio fire necessitated the rebuilding of all of the interior sets of the MacNeil house except for the bedroom. Blair and Burstyn were both hurt during filming—Burstyn's mishap resulted in a permanent spinal cord injury—and production delays added months to the shooting schedule. Friedkin reportedly asked for the set to be exorcised—which it was not—but the Reverend Thomas Bermingham, who was a technical advisor on the movie, did give the set a blessing.

A few last pieces of *Exorcist* trivia: The "Exorcist house" in which the MacNeils supposedly lived is located near the top of the staircase at 3600 Prospect Street NW. No scenes were shot inside the house. The building sits forty feet back from the stairs—much too far away to show Father Karras flying out of its second-story window and crashing onto the stairs below—so a façade of the house's east wall was built next to the steps. When it came time for the scene to be shot, enterprising Georgetown students charged people about five dollars to watch from an adjacent building and rooftops. Naturally, actor Jason Miller had a stunt double perform the fall. The staircase was covered with half-inch foam, and two takes were required to catch all the action.

Although not connected to *The Exorcist* story, there's a mansion that's reported to be haunted less than a block from the top of the notorious staircase. It stands to the east of the upper landing of the steps at 3508 Prospect Street NW and is known as Prospect House or Lingan-Templeman House. The residence, listed on the National Register of Historic Places, was built sometime between 1788 and 1793 by Brigadier General James MacCubin Lingan. An officer in the Continental Army during the American Revolution, Lingan went on to become a senior officer in the Maryland State Militia. He was killed by a mob in 1812 while trying to defend a friend's newspaper office in Baltimore. After Lingan's death, the house was sold to John Templeman, another member of Georgetown society.

The residence was eventually inherited by Mrs. Mary Steele Morris, who lived there from 1875 until her death in 1930. She owned the house when the "Exorcist steps" and city streetcar barn were constructed. Morris was a Spiritualist and frequently held séances in her dining room. She was also the first person to report paranormal activity inside Prospect House.

The initial spirit contact was a light rapping or scraping sound on one of the walls. Then, a piece of artwork that normally hung on the wall was discovered sitting on the floor. It had not fallen; the angled nail was still in place. Morris also sometimes heard muted, shuffling footsteps on the stairs leading to the third floor, as did a later tenant. One of Mrs. Morris's servants saw an unidentified apparition on the same staircase—that is, until the spectre vanished before the startled housekeeper's eyes.

And we can't leave the "Exorcist steps" without taking a look at the ghost legends of Georgetown University. Founded in 1789, it is the oldest Catholic and Jesuit university in the United States.

Healy Hall is the first building people see as they come through the school's main gates. Most of the structure was completed by 1879, and it was named to commemorate Father Patrick Francis Healy, who was the university president from 1873 to 1882. A former slave, Healy was the first African-American to head an American university.

Paul J. Pelz and John L. Smithmeyer, the same architects who designed the Library of Congress, were responsible for Healy Hall. The enormous, gray block building has been designated a National Historic Landmark and is on the National Register of Historic Places. And it's supposedly haunted.

For many years, there was a student tradition of stealing the hands from the massive clock on Healy Hall's tower and mailing them to the Vatican for a blessing. On one occasion around the turn of the twentieth century, a student fell while attempting the prank; other sources say he was moving the clock's hands to set the time. Regardless, the young man died, and his spectre has returned. The tower is now closed to students, but if anyone manages to get through all of the locked doors to the top, the student's ghost will act as a protector.

There's also a legend that the fifth floor leading to the clock tower has been sealed off because a former student inadvertently opened an entryway to the Other Side while chanting incoherent Latin phrases from an ancient, grimoire-like book he found in the university library. Unable to close the paranormal portal, the Jesuit fathers merely sealed off the area.

The oldest surviving building at Georgetown University is Old North, built in 1794. Like Healy Hall, it sits in the heart of campus on the old Quadrangle, whose other sides are bordered by Dahlgren Chapel and Ryan Hall. One of Old North's distinguishing characteristics is the octagonal garret at each end of the top floor. Known as "the towers," they were sometimes used to confine unruly students who were sent there to pray, ponder their actions, and repent. It's said that one of the pupils, unable to bear the humiliation of his punishment, leapt from one of the towers to his death. His ghost is now occasionally seen peering out of the towers' windows.

Finally, there's the matter of the Witch's Heads. During construction on campus in 1931, workers stumbled across a long-forgotten cemetery that turned out to have been an early burial grounds for Holy Trinity Church. While in use from 1818 to 1833, the graveyard was variously known as Trinity Burial Ground, Old Burial Ground, and College Ground.

A February 1939 article in *The Hoya*, the college newspaper, said that in the eighteenth century "the burial place was a playground of strange apparitions known as 'Witch's Heads.'" The strange "transparent, luminous globes" hovered over the graves, terrifying students. The paper suggested that the strange lights may have been caused by phosphorous gas seeping through the ground from poorly-embalmed, decomposing corpses.

Among those interred at the Old Burial Ground was Susan Decatur, the wife of naval hero Stephen Decatur. (See Chapter 9.) In 1953, her remains were moved to the nearby Holy Rook Cemetery, which the university also owned. Church and university records state that another "fifty bodies, more or less" were relocated from Trinity Burial Ground to Mount Olivet Cemetery in Maryland. Reiss Science Center now stands on the site of the former graveyard. There have been no reports of floating, incandescent orbs for more than a century.

Georgetown University is not the only haunted institution of higher learning in Washington, DC. Located in the city's northeast quadrant, Gallaudet University was the first post-secondary school in the world for the deaf and hard of hearing. Chartered by the federal government in 1856 and founded on land donated by former US Postmaster General Amos Kendall, Gallaudet University worked with the blind as well as the deaf until 1865. The institution acquired university status in 1986. The school's main building, House One, was originally the Victorian Gothic twenty-room residence of its first superintendent, Dr. Edward Miner Gallaudet. Legend has it that Gallaudet's ghost opens and shuts doors inside the building. His unseen spirit is also responsible for disembodied footsteps and rattling sounds, especially on the second floor.

Why do the "Exorcist steps" hold such fascination for fans of horror and the paranormal forty years after they came to national prominence?

In part, it's the visceral reaction people had when they saw the movie during its initial run. *The Exorcist* was released decades before the "slasher film" genre became commonplace. There had simply never been anything like it on the screen before.

The answer may also lie in everyone's inherent fear of the unknown, coupled with the unsettling suspicion that there are forces out there beyond their control wishing to do them harm.

A story such as *The Exorcist* forces us to examine our religious convictions. If we believe in survival of the spirit after death, can that essence, aura, or soul—call it what you will—return to and communicate or otherwise interact with those it left behind?

Most modern religions, while not promoting the existence of ghosts, take no definite stand against them either. There is nothing explicit on the subject in Catholic catechism, for example. Some other Christian sects, however, say that anything that materializes in the form of a deceased person—what we normally call a ghost—is a demon in disguise. The only true spirits are angels or other biblical figures, such as visitations by the Virgin Mary, known as Marian apparitions.

What do you believe in your heart of hearts? Do ghosts exist? And are there other kinds of spirits out there, good and evil? The Exorcist steps are a perfect place to contemplate such fundamental questions about what awaits us Beyond the Veil.

Part Five

THE REST OF THE STORY

You might think that with so many spectres haunting the White House, Capitol Hill, Lafayette Square, and Georgetown, that there couldn't possibly be any more apparitions lurking about the nation's capitol. But we've only just begun to scratch the surface.

The true number of spirits packed into the city's many nooks and crannies may never be known, but there are more than a dozen additional notable landmarks populated by otherworld entities. The locations are spread out all over the four quadrants of the district, ranging from private homes and hotels to government buildings, museums, and theaters—something of interest for every ghost hunt.

Chapter 20

The Lincoln Legacies

FORD'S THEATRE
511 10TH STREET NW

PETERSEN HOUSE
516 10TH STREET, NW

MARY SURRATT'S FORMER BOARDING HOUSE
604 H STREET NW

FORT LESLEY J. MCNAIR
4TH AND P STREETS SW

1ST STREET NE
CAPITOL HILL

The death of Abraham Lincoln had ramifications that John Wilkes Booth never could have imagined. The ghosts of at least four of the principal actors in the national calamity remain earthbound.

Everyone knows the story of how, on April 15, 1865, John Wilkes Booth crept up behind Abraham Lincoln in the Presidential Box at Ford's Theatre in Washington, DC, pointed his derringer at the back of the commander in chief's head, and took the life of the sixteenth president of the United States. What fewer people know are the plans leading up to the murder, why Booth had such extraordinary access to the president, and what happened to the others caught up in the unthinkable tragedy.

Junius Brutus Booth was a celebrated British Shakespearean actor who deserted his wife and moved to America with his mistress in 1821. He purchased a large farm outside of Bel Air, Maryland, where John Wilkes Booth, the ninth of his ten children, was born in 1838.

John and two of his older brothers, Junius Brutus Booth Jr. and Edwin, became actors like their father. John started reading Shakespeare and practicing elocution around the age of sixteen. He made his stage debut in a supporting role in an 1855 production of *Richard III* at the Charles Street Theatre in Baltimore. About the same time, he began acting at the nearby Holiday Street Theater, where his father and brother had appeared in productions for the playhouse's owner, John T. Ford.

Over the next few years, Booth became an accomplished actor, rivaling his brother Edwin's fame. Audiences—particularly ladies—loved John. Slim, athletic, and handsome, he had curly jet-black hair and stood five foot, eight inches tall. His performances were known for their physicality, especially when a role called for swordplay. He also got a reputation as a bit of a scene-stealer. Booth's success made him quite wealthy, too. When Ford opened a 1,500-seat theater in the heart of Washington, DC, John Wilkes Booth was one of the first leading men to appear there.

From the start, Booth was a supporter of the South's secession, but, with a few exceptions, he didn't share his sentiments with the general public. As his pro-slavery, anti-Union feelings deepened, he came to blame Lincoln—and Lincoln alone—for the war. The president's re-election in 1864 was more than the actor could bear. He came up with an audacious plan. He would kidnap Lincoln when the president went to stay at his summer residence, which was located about three miles from the White House on the grounds of the Soldiers' Home. Booth would then sneak Lincoln across the Potomac River to Richmond, Virginia, where he would turn over the president to the Confederate Army. As Booth finalized his plan, he gathered a group of coconspirators, including Samuel Arnold, David Herold, Michael O'Laughlen, George Atzerodt, Lewis Powell (also seen as Payne or Paine), and John Surratt Jr. They often met at the boarding house owned by Surratt's mother, Mary.

Mary Surratt is, perhaps, the most enigmatic figure in the whole affair. There's still debate as to how much she actually took part in the plans. Born Mary Jenkins, she married John Surratt, who had inherited farmland from his adoptive family, in 1840. It was not a happy union; John drank heavily and was prone to fits of temper. In 1853, John built an inn, which he called Surratt's Tavern, near Clinton, Maryland, about twelve miles outside of DC. After selling off some of his other property, Surratt was able to buy a townhouse on H Street in Washington, and he opened it to tenants.

The Surratts were Confederate sympathizers, and their tavern soon became a meetinghouse for spies, couriers, and the like. John Surratt died from a stroke on August 25th or 26th, 1862, leaving his family deep in debt. His son, John Jr., was unable to help out: He had recently lost his position as postmaster in the village near their tavern because federal officers were unsure of his loyalties. Unable to run the inn on her own, Mary Surratt leased it to a fellow Southern supporter, and between October and December 1864, she moved to the three-story townhouse in the city.

She immediately advertised for lodgers. Over the next year, her renters and guests included virtually every player in the Lincoln assassination. As President Andrew Johnson allegedly noted when he signed Mary Surratt's death warrant, she had "kept the nest that hatched the egg."

On March 4, 1865, Booth, Herold, Atzerodt, and Powell attended Lincoln's second inauguration, but they wisely didn't try to abduct the president that day. Instead, on March 17th, Booth and his crew waited along the road leading to the Soldiers' Home because they had heard Lincoln would be attending a play at a nearby hospital. Unfortunately for the schemers, the president changed his mind and never showed.

General Robert E. Lee surrendered to General Ulysses S. Grant at Appomattox Court House on April 12, 1865. The Civil War was over. Booth immediately changed his plan from kidnapping the president to killing him.

His chance came on April 14th—Good Friday. Booth stopped by Ford's Theatre that morning to pick up his mail. He heard from the owner's brother that President and Mrs. Lincoln would be attending a performance of *Our American Cousin* that evening with a guest: General Grant. Booth realized that if he struck that night, he might be able to eliminate both Lincoln and Grant.

Booth rushed to a nearby stable to secure a horse for his getaway. He called his fellow plotters together and gave them their new orders: Booth would go to the theater to shoot Lincoln and, if possible, Grant. At the same time, Atzerodt would kill Vice President Andrew Johnson and Powell would go to Lafayette Square to do the same to Secretary of State William Seward. Herold would assist with all of their escapes.

Atzerodt and Powell both failed in their missions. The former lost his nerve and went to a bar instead; Powell got as far as Seward's bedroom and slashed him in the face, but Seward's son and servant intervened, stopping the attack. In the scuffle, Powell escaped through the front door. Grant had decided not to go to the theater that night; Lincoln was not so lucky.

Booth not only knew Ford's Theatre intimately from working there, but he was well liked by the crew. He had free and total access to any area of the playhouse, at any time. When he returned to the theater that night, he quickly made his way unseen up a staircase that led from backstage to behind the Presidential Box. Having drilled a peephole in the door earlier in the day, Booth was able to ascertain the perfect time to slip in. He pulled out his gun, aimed point blank at the back of the president's head, and fired!

Major Henry Reed Rathbone, who had taken General Grant's place as the president's guest was in the box with his fiancée, Clara Harris. He attempted to grab the assassin, but Booth stabbed the officer. The actor then jumped down to the stage and famously cried, *"Sic semper tyrannis!"* ("Thus always to tyrants!") He rushed through the back door of the theater to the rear alley where his horse was waiting under the watchful eye of Edman Spangler, one of the theater's carpenters. (Booth had hired him, too, earlier that day.)

Booth galloped off and soon met up with Herold, and the two fled into Maryland. Around midnight they stopped at Surratt's Tavern to pick up guns and supplies that had been stashed there for them, possibly by Mary Surratt.

Around 4 a.m., Booth and Herold made an emergency stop at the home of Dr. Samuel Mudd. Booth had broken his left leg and needed to have it set. It's popularly believed that the injury occurred when Booth leapt to the stage, but Booth told the doctor he had been hurt when his horse fell out from under him.

(Mudd probably heard about the assassination later that day, but he didn't report Booth's visit to the authorities for another twenty-four hours. This, along with inconsistencies in his story and the fact he knew Booth and three of the coconspirators prior to the assassination, led to his being arrested for aiding and abetting Booth's escape.)

The president had been fatally wounded at 10:33 p.m. He was carried across the street to the Petersen boarding-house, taken upstairs, and made as comfortable as possible. After a grueling night, he died at 7:22 a.m.—making him the first US president to be assassinated.

Booth and Herold continued to travel into southern Maryland, where they hid in the dense forest and under-brush until it was safe to cross the Potomac River into Virginia. After a few false starts, they eventually succeeded on April 23rd and, with the help of local Confederate sympathizers, got to the farm of Richard H. Garrett, who let them hide in his tobacco barn under assumed names.

Aided by informants, the army had been closing in on Booth and Herold for days. They finally tracked them to the Garrett farm and surrounded the barn. Herold surrendered, but Booth refused. Under orders from Secretary of War Edwin Stanton to capture Booth alive, the soldiers set fire to the building in an attempt to force the murderer to come out. One of the men, Sergeant Boston Corbett, shot into the barn against orders and hit Booth in the back of the head, about an inch below the spot that Booth's bullet had entered President Lincoln. (Corbett later claimed self-defense, saying Booth had leveled his gun at him and was about to fire.)

Booth was pulled from the burning barn, mortally wounded. He died knowing that he had failed in his attempt to break the country's spirit and revive the Confederacy. He also knew that far from calling him a hero, most of the nation spurned his actions and reviled him—including the leading newspapers and many in the South. Even General Lee distanced himself from Booth's treachery.

According to the memoirs of Booth's sister, when the young man was thirteen he had visited a fortune teller on a lark. The seer told him that he was destined to have a momentous but short life and would be "meeting a bad end." Perhaps the Gypsy woman had actually been in tune with the spirits all those years ago.

Eight people were arrested for conspiracy in the Lincoln assassination and tried before a military commission. As Judge Advocate General of the US Army, Joseph Holt was the lead prosecutor.

On June 30, 1865, all of the defendants were pronounced guilty. Four were hanged in the Old Arsenal Penitentiary on July 7th: Powell, Atzerodt, Herold, and Mary Surratt—making her the first woman to be executed by the federal government.

Arnold, O'Laughlen, and Mudd were given life sentences; Spangler received a six-year sentence. O'Laughlen died of yellow fever in prison in 1867. President Johnson pardoned the remaining three in 1869.

John Surratt Jr. had managed to escape arrest and got to Canada. He made his way to Europe, but was finally arrested in Egypt in 1866. From there, he was extradited to the United States. By then, military trials for civilians had been declared unconstitutional, so he was tried in a regular court. Surratt confessed plotting to kidnap Lincoln in order to exchange him for Confederate prisoners of war, but he was found not guilty of being involved in the assassination. The statute of limitations for all of the other charges against him had run out, so he was set free.

Several ghost legends have grown up around this sprawling cast of characters.

Abraham Lincoln's spectre has appeared with some frequency at the White House and at least twice at the former Loudon Cottage in Connecticut. (The modest home belonged to the family of Clara Harris.) The president has also been said to manifest on rare occasions at the Petersen House.

On April 21, 1865, a train carrying Lincoln's body set out from Washington, DC, on a thirteen-day journey to Springfield, Illinois, where the slain leader would be buried. Every year on the same date the original cortège passed by, there are reports of people spotting the phantom of the funeral train along parts of the route, its cars silent and draped in black.

A few days after Lincoln's death, famed photographer Mathew Brady took several shots inside the auditorium of Ford's Theatre. When the photos were developed, a hazy figure resembling John Wilkes Booth was seen in a shot of the empty presidential box. Now, Spiritualism was in its heyday in the 1860s, and there were fraudulent mediums using double exposures to produce fake images of loved ones for their clients. For example, William H. Mumler, the discoverer of "spirit photography," shot a portrait of Mary Todd Lincoln with a cloudy image of the deceased president standing behind her. But Brady was no Mumler, and there's no easy explanation of how Booth's likeness showed up in one of his photos—unless, of course, ghosts really can be captured on film.

Congress forced the closure of Ford's Theatre after the assassination, and for many years the building was used for federal offices and storage. In 1968, it was refurbished and opened as a museum, administered by the National Park Service. But the theater is once again an active playhouse, and several staff members, tourists, and theatergoers have reported seeing Booth's translucent apparition throughout the building. His disembodied footsteps have been heard on the back staircase and behind the Presidential Box. Actors have felt an icy chill or cold spot—believed by paranormalists to be evidence of a spirit presence—when standing downstage, left of center, where Booth landed when he jumped from the Presidential Box. They've also experienced nausea, trembling, and anxiety or have forgotten their lines.

The former Surratt boardinghouse still stands about eight long blocks away. By the 1870s, it was common knowledge that the building was haunted. Anna, Mary's daughter, had moved from the townhouse after her mother's execution and sold it for next to nothing. (Today, Anna's ghost appears on the North Portico of the White House every year on the anniversary of the night before her mother was hanged.)

Subsequent owners and guests of the boarding house have reported hearing sobs and whispers, incorporeal footsteps, and creaking floors. Most of the activity took place on the second story, where Mary's bedroom was located. It was always assumed that the entity causing the phenomena was Mary Surratt. In 2009, the building was placed on the National Register of Historic Places. There have been few, if any, recent reports of ghost activity.

Mary Surratt also haunts the former Washington Arsenal, where she spent most of her incarceration and was executed. The military base, known as Fort Lesley J. McNair since 1948, was built at the confluence of the Potomac and Anacostia Rivers in 1794. Surratt's translucent wraith makes sporadic appearances in the area of the long-dismantled gallows.

Surratt would not recognize most of the former arsenal today. Ninety percent of the fort's buildings were remodeled or newly constructed in 1908. Her cell is said to have been in what is now Building 21. Disembodied footsteps and sobbing have been heard on an upper floor; so, too, has the rattling of one of the windows. The activity takes place most often in the month of April, when Surratt was hanged.

Surratt's ghost isn't the only apparition to haunt Fort Lesley J. McNair. From 1898 up to his death in 1902 at the age of fifty-one, Major Walter Reed headed an army hospital in the Washington Arsenal. (Reed is remembered for confirming the cause of yellow fever and coming up with an effective treatment.) The arsenal's hospital, a predecessor to Walter Reed Army Medical Center, closed in 1909, but legend has it that Reed's spectre continues to make rounds in the fort, walking corridors with his arms clasped behind his back.

The lonely phantom of an elderly man is sometimes seen walking along 1st Street NE on Capitol Hill, heading toward A Street NE, where the Old Capitol Prison once stood. The spectre, wearing a dark cape over a Civil War–era blue suit—some sources say it's a Union army uniform—is thought to be Judge Joseph Holt. The jurist was known by his friends, colleagues, and especially his neighbors to pace the sidewalk in front of his now-demolished residence at 236 New Jersey Avenue NW as he contemplated his cases.

After he retired, Holt seldom left the confines of his home, but in death his troubled spirit has apparently once again taken to the street. He's most often spied walking in the direction of A Street, so perhaps he's unaware that the Old Capitol Prison where Mary Surratt and Dr. Samuel Mudd (and, for a time, John T. Ford) were held was torn down years ago. It's now the site of the US Supreme Court.

Finally, there's the peripheral haunting associated with the attempt of William Seward's life that was discussed in Chapter 11. As Powell crept through Seward's home, intent on murdering the secretary of state, a loud, cacophonous noise alerted Seward's son and the housekeeper that something was amiss. The myth emerged that the ghost of Philip Barton Key, who had been gunned down outside the house six years earlier, had caused the racket because he didn't want to see another defenseless killing on Lafayette Square.

Chapter 21

Do Not Disturb

SITE OF THE COLONEL BEAU HICKMAN HAUNTINGS
6TH STREET AND PENNSYLVANIA AVENUE NW

Was it being disinterred by grave robbers or wanting to rejoin his friends in a game of poker that caused gambler Beau Hickman to return from the Other Side to walk the streets of Washington, DC?

There are few characters in the history of nineteenth century Washington more flamboyant than Colonel Beau Hickman, but because he wasn't involved in business, politics, or the military—his title "Colonel" was an honorary one, possibly self-adopted—he has largely been forgotten.

Hickman was born in Virginia of prosperous parents in 1813. In either 1833 or 1834, he moved to the District of Columbia to make his mark on the world. He had no trade, but he was young, handsome, wealthy, charming, witty—all of the makings of a *bon vivant*. He quickly endeared himself to society and was soon spending lavishly and attending the best parties on the arms of beautiful women. Rather than settling into a house, he chose to stay in hotels, where he could mingle with guests, meet with friends, and make new ones in the elegant lobbies. His favorite haunt was the five-story National Hotel at the corner of 6th Street and Pennsylvania Avenue NW.

Hickman's expensive tastes and lavish living belied the fact that he was often near destitute. He had come to the city with a reported $10,000 from his family, but he went through that within two years. Fortunately, he did have a way of making money, however dubious: He was an excellent, if uneven, gambler. His particular talent was with a deck of cards.

Like any in his field, he had his good days and bad days, but he never lost a friend or made an enemy over a round of poker. He was scrupulously honest, a generous winner, and gracious in defeat. His pals also knew that if Hickman lost, he was good for his debts—if not always in money, then in affable companionship. Most of all, people just liked Hickman, and it served him well. For example, one time when he ran short of money at the Metropolitan Hotel, instead of throwing him out on his ear, the management gently (but firmly) suggested he might prefer the accommodations across the street at the even more expensive National Hotel. With nothing to lose, Hickman tried his luck, and the National gave him a several-month's lease without question. (Current thought is that the hotel may have mistaken "Colonel" Hickman for a renowned Confederate General John Hickman.)

Hickman always seemed to float above the fray and everyday cares of the world. As a result, he acquired a nickname: the Prince of the American Bummers—"bummer" being slang at the time for a person who gets through life without a job and no real aim or purpose.

Hickman had lived such a extravagant life that his friends were stunned when they found out he had died penniless. In August 1873, Hickman was struck with "paralysis"—probably a stroke—and he was moved from his hotel to Providence Hospital. He died there on September 1st. According to popular belief, Hickman had been living at the National Hotel at the time, but given his financial situation, it's more likely he was in one of the cheap rooming houses in the area. Hickman was, quite literally, dead broke, and he was buried in Potter's Field.

When his friends heard that Hickman had been interred in a pauper's grave, they decided their comrade deserved a better resting place: He should be in Congressional Cemetery!

A near-contemporary report by James Samuel Trout says that Hickman's friends took up a collection the day after his burial to pay for the re-interment. They also arranged carriages at the various hotels that Hickman often visted for anyone who wanted to attend the exhumation and funeral at the new cemetery.

No one was prepared for what they discovered when the body was removed from the ground. Grave robbers had broken into Hickman's coffin, cut him open, and removed his brain and heart—undoubtedly to sell to a medical school. The way in which the broken coffin and mutilated corpse had been hastily reburied suggested that the looters had been discovered in the act. Though appalled at the desecration of the body, Hickman's friends completed their mission by moving his remains to Congressional Cemetery and performing last rites.

Legend tells a much more festive tale: After a few drinks, Hickman's mates decided to sneak into the beggar's graveyard to steal his body and move it under cover of night. In this version of the story, they found Hickman's body halfway out of the ground, abandoned by the body snatchers after they had done their gruesome work. Hickman's friends loaded the shrouded, defiled cadaver into the back of their wagon and hauled it over to Congressional Cemetery. They quickly dug a hole, lowered Hickman into the ground, filled in the grave, and marked it with a make-shift tombstone. After a quick prayer, they hurried off.

Regardless of which story is correct, it was shortly after Hickman's body was moved that strange things—what, today, we would call paranormal activity—started happening during card games back at the hotels he had frequented, especially if any of Hickman's old cronies were playing. Soon, people began seeing Beau Hickman's ghost, replete with his trademark beaver hat, diamond stickpin, and cane, strolling on the sidewalk outside of the National Hotel.

The street corner where the hotel was located is now the site of Newseum, the Freedom Forum's museum of journalism. It's only two blocks north of the National Gallery of Art and the National Mall and about a half-mile northwest of the US Capitol. If some night you're in the neighborhood and you see a lonely figure wearing what seems to be nineteenth-century garb at 6th and Pennsylvania, take a closer look. It might be the colonel seeking a new player to ante in.

Chapter 22

Dead Letter Office

THE OLD POST OFFICE PAVILION
1100 PENNSYLVANIA AVENUE NW

There have been calls to tear down the Old Post Office almost since it opened. But a major real estate deal has given it a new lease on life. Maybe the building's many ghosts, who seem to have been dormant for a number of years, will come back to play.

By the end of the nineteenth century, Washington, DC, was long overdue for a new post office. Congress approved construction of one in June 1890 on a site in the disreputable part of the city known as Murder Bay. The hope was that a legitimate business in the area (now called the Federal Triangle) might help clean up the petty crime and prostitution in the neighborhood and revitalize the community.

Construction on the Romanesque Revival building started in 1892. It took seven years and three million dollars to complete the superstructure, which included a massive 315-foot-tall clock tower soaring overhead. Even today the tower is the third tallest structure in Washington. There's an observation deck at the 270-foot level that has a commanding view of the city, and below that on the tenth floor are the Bells of Congress—replicas of the bells found at Westminster Abbey in London. They were a bicentennial gift from the Ditchley Foundation in England.

The tower has held up well since its inauguration with one hiccup: The clock (which has a dial on each of the tower's four sides) was originally run by gravity using a long cable wrapped around a circular drum and bearing a heavy weight. On October 10, 1956, the weight snapped off the cable and fell two stories, almost killing a man who had just left his desk. Soon after, the clock was replaced with a model powered by electricity.

The main section of what's now known as the Post Office Pavilion originally had ten floors of balconies surrounding a central, 196-foot-high atrium—the largest open, enclosed space in the city at the time. The building had several wrought-iron elevators and was the first major structure in Washington to have all of its electrical wiring built inside its walls.

Unfortunately, by the time the building opened, advances in architecture had already made it out of date. Plus, the construction had been poor to begin with: There were leaky windows, drafts, and uneven marble floors. In fact, some of the floors couldn't bear the weight for which they were intended. Add to that, many people—including some of the country's top architects—simply found the building ugly.

The real problem was that the building was too small for all of the government offices that were supposed to move into it—including its main tenant, the post office. During the design period, the local postmaster said that 50,000 square feet were needed to process all of the city's mail. He got 10,000. In 1914, the post office gave up trying to make do and moved to a new facility. People began to refer to the building on Pennsylvania Avenue as the "Old Post Office."

Other agencies stayed in the building, and it has never sat empty. But there have been calls to raze the structure in every decade of its existence. At first the building was too new to justify its destruction; then the Depression made its demolition a political non-starter. By the 1950s, the pavilion and tower were gaining iconic status, and preservationists started a movement to save it in the 1970s. Then, in 1973, the Old Post Office was added to the National Directory of Historic Places.

An eighteen-million-dollar renovation by the Government Services Administration began in 1977, and Vice President George H. W. Bush rededicated the building and tower in April 1983. In addition to offices, the modernized facility contained restaurants, retail space, and a small performance center. Still, the building was a losing proposition for merchants. Tenancy declined throughout the 1990s, and by 2004 costly repairs were once again needed. In June 2013, after more than a year of negotiations, the GSA announced a sixty-year lease agreement with the Trump Organization, which plans to transform the property into a hotel with approximately 260 rooms. As part of the arrangement, the public will still have access to the historic clock tower, with tours conducted by the National Park Service.

There were claims of a ghost or ghosts haunting the Old Post Office Pavilion as early as the turn of the twentieth century. Most of the reports centered on the elevators located in the main building. No one ever saw an apparition there, but the lifts would open between floors or stop at ones where they hadn't been called. There were also plenty of false alarms that passengers were trapped inside the elevators.

It's thought that the ghostly shenanigans may have been caused by James P. Willett, who was the District of Columbia postmaster when the Post Office Pavilion opened. On September 30, 1899, he plummeted a hundred feet to his death down an elevator shaft. What caused him to stumble and fall is unknown—he may have had a stroke—but at the time there was only a temporary wooden barricade blocking the open shaft rather than the regular door.

The other paranormal phenomena took place inside the clock tower: The bells rang by themselves in the middle of the night. Whenever watchmen investigated, the bells and ropes were swinging, but the chamber in which they were housed was otherwise empty. There's an old wives' tale that on one occasion a pair of guards went into the bell room to look into the clamor and were shocked to see the spectre of a man in a long coat and black boots standing there. They couldn't identify the apparition, but, then, they didn't have much time to try. As they watched, the phantom disappeared. Within moments, the two men were running down the staircase and out of the building.

It's uncertain whether the hauntings are still going on. Visits to the Old Post Office Tower were suspended in 2014 until the completion of the hotel complex. Both the hotel and tower are slated to open sometime in 2016 as this book goes to press. Will some otherworldly essence return to jinx the new elevators or signal their presence in the clock tower? Only time will tell.

Chapter 23
Abandon All Hope

EMBASSY OF THE REPUBLIC OF INDONESIA
2020 MASSACHUSETTS AVENUE NW

SMITHSONIAN INSTITUTION BUILDING
1000 JEFFERSON DRIVE SW

INDEPENDENCE AVENUE
BETWEEN 7TH AND 9TH STREETS SW

Taken separately, these next three ghost stories seem to have little in common. Combine them with the curse of the Hope Diamond, however, and you have a tale that could only take place in Washington, DC.

Our tale begins in 1860, when Thomas J. Walsh emigrated to the United Sated from Ireland. Poor but resourceful, Walsh worked hard in a variety of jobs and invested his money well, but he lost almost all of his savings in the Panic of 1893. He moved to Colorado three years later and, with the remainder of his fortune, bought Camp Bird Mine, a silver mine that most people thought was depleted. They were wrong. Instead, Walsh struck it rich when gold was discovered . . . and then more silver! Walsh sold the mine in 1902 for $5.2 million.

In 1898, he had moved his family, which included daughter Evalyn and son Vinson, to Washington, DC. They then spent two years in Paris before returning to the District of Columbia for good. That's when Walsh began building his showcase mansion in the DuPont Circle neighborhood.

When construction was completed in 1903, the house had sixty rooms, a grand staircase, a French salon, a ballroom, and a theater. It cost $835,000, making it the most expensive private residence in DC up to that time. Walsh spent another two million over the next few years lavishly furnishing the interior.

In 1908, Evalyn married Edward Beale "Ned" McLean, the heir to a publishing dynasty, whose holdings included the *Washington Post*. (Ned was the newspaper's owner and publisher from 1916 to 1941.) Although the couple had their own homes elsewhere in the city, after Evalyn's father died in 1910, she and Ned also occupied the Walsh Mansion. In 1911, after a year of negotiations with Pierre Cartier, the McLeans purchased the already-famous Hope Diamond.

Evalyn Walsh McLean died in 1947. (Her husband had predeceased her in 1941.) Despite all of her fabulous possessions, the family was deeply in debt. In 1952, the estate sold the Walsh Mansion to the Republic of Indonesia, which made it their Washington embassy.

Evalyn had been seventeen when the family moved into their magnificent home on Massachusetts Avenue. She was sixty at the time of her death. That's a lot of time to fall in love with your surroundings. Evalyn is buried in nearby Rock Creek Cemetery, but apparently the socialite's spirit has never left her manse. Every now and then, embassy staff and visitors see her apparition float down the central staircase. If reports are true, she occasionally does it in the nude!

As for the Hope Diamond, by the time Evalyn Walsh McLean bought it, she must have been aware that there was a curse attached to the 45-carat gemstone: Supposedly, death and disaster would befall anyone who owned the precious jewel.

Since any curse would have to be carried out by spirits of some sort, it's worth taking a brief look at the story of the Hope Diamond. In 1653, Jean Baptiste-Tavernier, a French gem merchant, purchased the gigantic stone in India. Some reports say he actually stole it from a statue in a Hindu shrine, so the temple priests laid a curse on the diamond. Regardless, the jewel, which soon became known as the Tavernier Blue, passed through the hands of many owners in several countries. At one point it was being called the French Blue.

Along the way, the diamond was reshaped and cut into smaller pieces. By the time the largest extant chuck made its way into the hands of Evalyn Walsh McLean it was known as the Hope Diamond, having gotten that name when the Hope banking family in England owned it. Evalyn bequeathed it to her grandchildren, but trustees of her estate sold the stone to New York jeweler Harry Winston in 1949 to pay off debts. In 1958, Winston was persuaded to donate the Hope Diamond to the Smithsonian Institution, where it would become the centerpiece of a new national gem collection to be housed in the Museum of Natural History.

So how about that curse? Did anyone ever suffer a hardship or get hurt after obtaining the prized jewel?

According to legend, Baptiste-Tavernier almost died of fever after buying (or stealing) the massive rock. But he was traveling in India in the 1600s, so he could simply have picked up a bug along the way. King Louis XIV, who had it for a time, died of gangrene, and all but one of his children died before becoming adults. Things didn't end so well for its next owners—Louis XVI and Marie Antoinette. Then there was Wilhelm Fals, a Dutch jeweler, one of the many people who recut the diamond. He was murdered by his son, who then killed himself. And how about Simon Maoncharides, a Greek merchant who also may have owned the stone? He drove off a cliff, taking his wife and child with him. Within nine months of delivering the Hope Diamond to the Smithsonian Institution, postman James Todd broke his leg in a truck accident, suffered a head injury in a second accident, and had his house burn to the ground.

All in all, there were about a dozen people who ran into, shall we say, bad luck after being directly or even tangentially associated with the Hope Diamond. But what about our restless spirit, Evalyn Walsh McLean, who still haunts her former abode? What misfortunes, if any, befell her after she purchased the stone?

Well, her nine-year-old son died after being struck by a car, her daughter died at twenty-five from an overdose of sleeping pills, her husband had at least one adulterous affair, and he eventually had to be committed to a mental asylum, where he died.

The Natural History Museum, where the Hope Diamond remains on display, is part of the Smithsonian Institution. One of Washington's most interesting hauntings took place for about a decade in the institution's first building, which is nicknamed the Castle.

James Smithson, an English scientist, was born James Lewis Mace in 1765. His mother was widowed at the time of his birth, and he found out years later that he was illegitimate. His true father was Hugh Smithson, the Duke of Northumberland, who acknowledged James as his son.

James attended Oxford, was made a fellow of the Royal Society, and devoted his life to the study of minerals. He died in Genoa, Italy, in 1829.

It's unknown why Smithson, who never visited America, would bequeath his fortune—a half-million dollars—to the United States for the express purpose of constructing a national museum. Amazingly, it took Congress eight years to accept the gift, and the institution wasn't chartered until 1846.

The original Smithsonian Institution Building (the Castle) was constructed between 1847 and 1855. Until 1881, all of the museum's operations were housed there. Today it's the museum's administrative center—except for a crypt on the ground floor.

Smithson had been buried in the Genoan-English Cemetery, but in the early part of the twentieth century a company that operated marble quarries bought the graveyard and turned it into an excavation site. The firm relocated all of the graves, and Smithson's remains were brought to the United States. A guardroom just inside the Castle entranceway was converted into a tomb, and Smithson's sarcophagus was placed there.

In the 1970s, strange things began to happen in the Castle. A female visitor had an invisible hand grab her necklace from behind, then let it fall back onto her neck. Books fell from the shelves of the Woodrow Wilson Library on the third floor. The elevator would stop or its alarms would go off for no reason. Workers in the middle of the night felt they were being watched.

Then, during a renovation in the late 1970s, Smithson's sarcophagus was opened. It was discovered that, rather than being properly laid out, his bones, fragments of the original coffin, and its nameplate had been tossed together in a tin box helter-skelter. Once the bones were correctly arranged, and the crypt resealed, the hauntings stopped.

Finally, an infamous haunted site is located directly behind the Hirshhorn Museum and Sculpture Garden. The art museum, also part of the Smithsonian Institution, was endowed in the 1960s and contains the collection of Joseph J. Hirshhorn. Its focus is modern art, particularly post-World War II pieces.

The museum's front door opens onto the National Mall, but its back façade faces Independence Avenue. Before the Emancipation Proclamation was signed, slaves who were about to be auctioned in DC were held in two notorious prisons located near the 800 block of Independence Avenue: the Yellow House (also known as the Williams Slave Pen) and Robey Slave Pen.

There's been renewed interest in the holding yards since the release of the 2013 movie *Twelve Years a Slave*. Solomon Northrup, the film's lead character, was a free black man who was nonetheless kidnapped and sold into slavery. It's believed that he was kept for a time in the Yellow House.

The inhumane Williams and Robey slave pens were torn down more than a century ago, and the men, women, and children that were held there against their will have surely Crossed Over. But today, people walking along the stretch of Independence Avenue between 7th and 9th Streets sometimes hear the captives' ghostly screams and the clanking of invisible iron chains, especially at night.

All of the hauntings in these four intertwined tales have taken place within a few short miles of one other. Sounds like a good excuse for a road trip.

Chapter 24

The Ghost Suites

WILLARD INTERCONTINENTAL HOTEL
1401 PENNSYLVANIA AVENUE NW

MAYFLOWER HOTEL
1127 CONNECTICUT AVENUE NW

OMNI SHOREHAM HOTEL
2500 CALVERT STREET NW

What do the Willard, the Mayflower, and the Shoreham have in common? Well, obviously they're all hotels, and they're all in Washington, DC. But they're all also haunted, even though their stories are unique.

In 1816, Colonel John Tayloe III, the same man who built the now-haunted Octagon House, constructed six small houses on Pennsylvania Avenue. The units were leased to a number of folks over the next thirty years who operated the houses collectively as a hotel. In 1847, Henry Willard rented them from Tayloe's son, Benjamin Ogle Tayloe, and converted them into a single four-story structure that he named the Willard Hotel. He bought the property outright in 1864, and the hotel stood there until 1901, when it was replaced by the current twelve-story building.

The Willards sold their stock in the hotel in 1948, and a number of factors led to the facility's being closed in 1968.

It remained unoccupied for many years until the InterContinental Hotel Group became interested in the property. The developers restored the hotel's turn-of-the-twentieth century elegance and reopened it in 1986. Today, the hotel is officially known as The Willard InterContinental Hotel, but everyone simply calls it "the Willard."

The Willard is centrally located in the heart of Washington, one block east of the west wing of the White House, so everyone who is anyone in DC politics has passed through its doors. Abraham Lincoln, who was a personal friend of Henry Willard, stayed there for a week with his family prior to his first inauguration. Sadly, Lincoln had to be slipped into the hotel secretly because he was already receiving death threats because of his anti-slavery views. It's said that Lincoln, who referred to himself as a simple "prairie lawyer," was so short of funds that he couldn't cover his bill when he checked out; he had to wait until he received his first paycheck as president.

The Willard Hotel became a favorite of President Ulysses S. Grant. He used to take an early evening stroll to the hotel, where he would sit in the lobby, enjoy a cigar and brandy, and watch people come and go. When his almost-daily habit became known, those who wanted to ask favors or press their points of view on pending legislation would show up in the lobby to meet him. Grant began to call these people "lobbyists"—a term that has stuck to this day.

Modern guests often say they feel Grant's presence as they pass through the foyer. They also sometimes catch a whiff of the president's cigar when no one is smoking nearby. Today, there's no smoking permitted in the lobby, so if you smell the scent of a fine cigar, look around. The great Civil War general and eighteenth president might be looking over your shoulder.

The next of our haunted sites to come on the scene was the Mayflower Hotel. Construction on what was to have been called the Hotel Walker (after owner Allen E. Walker) began in July 1922. By the time of its completion, Walker had sold his shares to C.C. Mitchell & Company, another major developer. The firm renamed the building the Mayflower Hotel in commemoration of the 300th anniversary of the *Mayflower*'s landing at Plymouth Rock.

The ten-story hotel opened to the public in 1925. Costing roughly eleven million dollars to complete, it's often referred to as the "Grande Dame of Washington, DC." Another of its nicknames, the city's "Second Best Address"—after that of the White House, of course—supposedly came from President Harry Truman, who stayed at the Mayflower numerous times.

The hotel's interior is filled with antique and reproduction furnishings, marble statuary, and other artwork. It's thought that there is more gold leaf on the first floor and mezzanine than in any other building in Washington except for the Library of Congress. The hotel has at least 500 guest rooms and almost seventy suites, including two presidential suites. The building has been named a US Historic Site and is listed on the US National Register of Historic Places.

The hotel has undergone several changes in ownership, the most recognizable names being the Hilton Corporation, Stouffer Hotels, Renaissance Hotels, and its current proprietor, Marriott International.

The "Hotel of Presidents," as the Mayflower Hotel is also known, was the site of Calvin Coolidge's inaugural ball in

1925. Coolidge had been elected vice president under Warren G. Harding in 1920 and assumed the presidency after the latter's unexpected death in 1923. Coolidge was elected president in his own right in 1924 after campaigning as a conservative who favored a small federal government.

He acquired the sobriquet "Silent Cal" during his vice presidency due to his tendency to say very little when not making public addresses. When he did speak, he often showed a sly sense of humor. There's an oft-told story, possibly apocryphal, about an exchange that took place at a Washington dinner party attended by the president. A woman seated next to Coolidge told him that she had bet someone she could get more than two words out of him. He allegedly replied, "You lose."

Coolidge's younger son, Calvin, died in July 1924 during the president's election campaign. Coolidge was heartbroken. He was quoted as saying that when his son died "the power and glory of the Presidency went with him," but Coolidge was obliged to continue on the road to woo voters. He won the election and then presided over the period of economic growth known as "the Roaring Twenties." He died at "The Beeches," his home in Northampton, Massachusetts, on January 5, 1933.

Coolidge didn't attend the inaugural festivities held in his honor at the Mayflower Hotel on January 20, 1925. He was still in mourning for his son. Now, every year on that date, the lights in the hotel mysteriously flicker and dim on their own at 10 p.m.—the very time that Coolidge was scheduled to enter the ballroom! Also, an elevator sticks on the eighth floor for fifteen minutes when the president would have been descending to the gala from his suite upstairs. Is the ghost of the former commander in chief causing the eerie phenomena? It's a pretty good guess, but no one knows for sure.

The Mayflower isn't the only Washington hotel to hold inaugural galas. The Shoreham Hotel, now the Omni Shoreham, hosted the first presidential party for Franklin Delano Roosevelt in 1933, and it has held an inaugural ball for every president since. Bill Clinton famously played the saxophone at his Shoreham Hotel gala in 1993.

The Shoreham was built in 1930 by a local developer, Harry Bralove. One of the minority stakeholders in the hotel was financier Henry Doherty. Shortly after the Shoreham Hotel opened, Doherty and his family moved into one of its eighth-floor apartments. A few months later, their maid, Juliette Brown, suddenly and inexplicably died in her room in the middle of the night. Shortly thereafter, Doherty's daughter Helen died in the apartment as well. Without explanation, Doherty and his wife moved out, and no one lived in the suite for years—in part because of rumors that the apartment was haunted.

Once people began renting the rooms again, the stories turned out to be true! Occupants complained about the lights and TVs turning themselves on. Doors would slam shut. Guests would hear barely audible whispers and feel unexplainable cold breezes in the rooms. They'd come back to discover the furniture had been rearranged while they were out. Housekeepers' carts moved without being touched. People staying in the adjacent suites would complain about indiscernible sounds coming from the rooms, even when they were empty. The former Doherty apartment, which became known as the "Ghost Suite," is now Suite 870.

Many haunted locations can't be visited because they're privately owned and closed to the public. But you're in luck. All you have to do to check out the ghosts at the Willard, the Mayflower, and the Shoreham is check in.

Chapter 25

Meigs Old Red Barn

NATIONAL BUILDING MUSEUM
401 F Street NW

A building can be repurposed, but that doesn't mean phantoms from its past don't linger. A popular museum in the nation's capital may have ghosts on display dating all the way back to its time as the Pension Building in the 1800s.

Congress created the private, non-profit National Building Museum in 1980 to celebrate architecture, design, construction, and urban planning. It's located in the northwest section of Washington, DC, inside a historic structure built to house the Pension Bureau. (Commissioned to handle pensions for Civil War veterans, their dependents, and survivors, the Pension Bureau was the first department of veterans' affairs.)

Construction of the Italian Renaissance–style building, designed by US Army Quartermaster General Montgomery C. Meigs, took place from 1882 to 1887. Built on the site of an old jail and an insane asylum, the building covers an entire city block, bordered by 4th, 5th, F, and G Streets. It soon acquired a nickname: "Meigs Old Red Barn."

The enormous structure required fifteen million red bricks to build. A frieze of twenty-eight continuous panels that depict Civil War soldiers wraps around the exterior of the building. Inside, its Great Hall, surrounded by arched galleries, measures an astounding 36,656 square feet. Eight massive Corinthian columns, each one towering seventy-five feet and measuring eight feet in diameter, divide the room into sections.

Meigs had wanted solid black onyx for the columns, but the material was prohibitively expensive. He finally found a Canadian artist who was able to produce a convincing faux-onyx finish. Meigs also had to compromise because of the weight: The pillars had to be hollow, which gave rise to a rumor that he stuffed the columns with confidential government documents and other relics.

It's also said that Robert Todd Lincoln, the president's son, did his own investigation into the assassination of his father. He supposedly came up with information that was so incendiary he asked Meigs to hide his papers inside one of the columns. As secretary of war under James A. Garfield, Robert Lincoln would have known Meigs, and he very well may have been the one to approve Meigs's blueprints for the Pension Building.

(It's not a ghost story, but here's something spooky: Robert Todd Lincoln was almost within shouting distance of three presidential assassinations. His parents had invited him to go with them to Ford's Theatre, but having just arrived in town, he begged off. He was at his father's bedside the next morning, however, when the Great Emancipator died. On July 2, 1881, Robert Lincoln was supposed to travel to New Jersey with President Garfield. Before they could board the train, the president was shot by Charles Guiteau. Then in 1901, Robert Lincoln traveled to Buffalo, New York, to attend the Pan American Exposition at the invitation of President William McKinley. Robert arrived late; otherwise he probably would have been with the president when anarchist Leon Czolgosz shot him. As a result,

Lincoln's son swore to stay away from any event that would be attended by an American president.)

By the 1960s, the seventy-year-old Pension Building was being occupied by several government departments. The edifice was showing its age, and rather than refurbish it, many people felt it should be demolished. Conservationists intervened, and Congress asked architect Chloethiel Wood Smith to investigate other possible uses for the building.

Born Chloethiel Blanche Woodard in 1910, Smith was already an up-and-coming designer by the time she moved to DC around 1935. She was one of the first women to be nationally recognized as an architect, and the bulk of her work was in Washington. She was at the top of her game in 1967 when she made the provocative suggestion that the government convert the former Pension Building into a museum dedicated to the art and craft of design and construction. It took thirteen years for that dream to become a reality. In the meantime, in 1969, the structure was placed on the US National Register of Historic Places. The building was officially named the National Building Museum in 1997.

Modern-day visitors who come to view the building's exhibits aren't alone. Ghosts have been reported there for a hundred years. The first recorded sighting dates to 1917 when a guard saw the swirling designs in the faux onyx near the top of one of the columns take the shape of an American Indian and the head of a buffalo. (Perhaps it was a coincidence that Wild West showman Buffalo Bill Cody, who had recently attended President Cleveland's inaugural ball inside the building, died that very evening.)

Before long, other people were seeing images in the whorls, too, such as (according to a newspaper at the time) "a malevolent grinning skull" and human faces—including those of George and Martha Washington.

In part to stop people's claims that unearthly faces were appearing on the columns, the pillars were covered over in the 1970s when the Pension Building became the Superior Court of the District of Columbia. But that didn't stop the other hauntings.

In the 1940s, evening guards said they saw a military man in uniform riding a horse on one of the upper levels. Some were convinced the rider was Montgomery Meigs himself. (Allegedly horses were sometimes stabled upstairs during the early years of the Pension Building, despite the difficulty in being able to safely guide them up or down steps.)

In 1972, a night watchman sitting at the Pension Building's first floor information desk saw the shadowy figure of a limping man, dressed in a light-colored suit, head for the main staircase. He followed the stranger up to the third floor. When the guard was finally able to see the phantom's face, he screamed and ran from the building. The man was later found wandering Pennsylvania Avenue in a daze. He told his supervisor and a doctor treating him that he had seen the fires of hell: The wraith he had encountered had no eyes and smelled of death. The guard was committed to a psychiatric hospital for treatment.

Those familiar with the building's history suggest that, because of the apparition's distinctive walk, the guard may have seen James Tanner, an early commissioner of pensions. As a corporal in the army, Tanner had lost both legs in the Second Battle of Bull Run. He then became a stenographer for the Bureau of Ordinance. On April 14, 1865, he was abruptly called to the Petersen House across from Ford's

Theatre. As Abraham Lincoln lay upstairs dying, Tanner's job was to take testimony from witnesses of the assassination and about the failed attempt on William Seward's life.

Years later, Tanner became a strong advocate for veterans' rights, which led to his being appointed pension commissioner in 1889. His tenure was short, however: He was relieved for raising veterans' benefits without authorization. He went on to become a successful pension attorney. Probably some of the old wives' tales about Tanner and Robert Lincoln have merged, because it's been suggested that Tanner's ghost returns to the Pension Building to find Robert Lincoln's documents about the president's assassination.

Now the National Building Museum, the site is one of the few places in Washington to embrace its haunted legends. In recent years, it's even offered ghost-themed tours during the Halloween season. Check their October schedule and make a reservation. If you're lucky, the spirits will be as curious about you as you are about them, and they'll come out of hiding to greet you.

Chapter 26

Final Curtain

NATIONAL THEATRE
1321 Pennsylvania Avenue NW

*There's always a question when a haunted structure is razed
whether its ghost will depart or move into whatever replaces it. The
National Theatre was rebuilt several times, but it always remained
a playhouse. Maybe that's why its phantom, who was an actor,
feels right at home.*

Washington has had a National Theatre for almost two
hundred years. In September 1834, a local mover-and-
shaker named William Wilson Corcoran gathered together
a like-minded group of citizens to discuss the construction
of a first-class playhouse for the city's social and political
elite. On December 7, 1835, their vision bore fruit when the
National Theatre welcomed its first patrons.

The playhouse sits on Pennsylvania Avenue, three long
blocks from the White House. Despite its name, the theater
has never been operated or funded by the federal government.
It's remained a private enterprise and has undergone changes
in ownership. For example, for a few years it was known as
Grover's National Theatre or simply Grover's Theatre to reflect
the name of its proprietor at the time, Leonard Grover.

The National Theatre suffered five fires in the nineteenth century. After each one, it had to be rebuilt and
refurbished. The last major renovation, from 1982 to 1983,
completely replaced the dressing room wing as part of

a major downtown redevelopment project. President and Nancy Reagan attended a performance of *42nd Street* as part of the theater's gala reopening in 1984. (It's believed that every president since Andrew Jackson has attended a performance at the National.)

The exterior of the seven-story building has almost no ornamentation. Other than the marquee out front, there's little to suggest that there's a playhouse inside. The graceful auditorium, which seats 1,676 audience members, features a domed ceiling and cerulean blue walls, which were originally decorated with allegorical murals. The wooden fronts of the box seats were carved with scenes of historical events, and the proscenium arch is topped by a depiction of the Declaration of Independence. The original main curtain displayed a painting of George Washington on horseback with Mount Vernon in the distance.

From its very beginning, the National Theatre attracted the major artists of the day. In the 1850s, Jenny Lind, the Swedish Nightingale brought to America by P. T. Barnum, played the National on her North American tour. President Abraham Lincoln saw John Wilkes Booth make his Washington debut in a production of Shakespeare's *Richard III* at the National. John Philip Sousa often conducted on the stage from 1882 to 1916, both as the head of The President's Own United States Marine Band and, later, the maestro's concert band. Flo Ziegfeld made the National Theatre the DC home of his Follies from 1907 to 1926. The stage has also presented the out-of-town tryouts of several Broadway shows, including the world premieres of two musical classics: *Show Boat* and *West Side Story*. A full list of the performers who have played the National would read like a *Who's Who* of the theater profession.

The actor who's appeared most often has been doing so for more than a hundred years. His name is John McCullough, and according to an old wives' tale, he was shot on the stage in the mid-1880s by one of his fellow thespians and buried in the theater's basement—directly below the spot where he fell. (Some say the entire company helped dispose of McCullough's body.) A rusty, Civil War–era gun, thought to have belonged to the killer, was found in the substructure during the building's makeover in 1982. Word is mixed on whether the excavations turned up any bones.

A variation of the story says that, at the time of the assault, McCullough and his assailant were washing their clothes in Tiber Creek, which ran through the basement. (The rivulet is still present far below the theater's foundation.)

Either version makes a good story, but McCullough actually died of general paresis in a Philadelphia asylum on November 8, 1885, at the age of fifty-two. His health had declined steadily after suffering a debilitating attack onstage the previous year in Chicago. Actors staged a benefit performance of *The Apostate* for McCullough at Ford's Theatre in March 1885. John Wilkes Booth was among its cast. McCullough is buried in Mount Moriah Cemetery in Philadelphia, and friends raised a granite monument with a massive bronze bust of the actor over his family plot.

Regardless of where McCullough died and is buried, there's no reason why his spirit wouldn't choose to return to the National Theatre. He was one of nineteenth-century America's most celebrated Shakespearean tragic actors, and he had appeared on the stage at the National Theatre many times, beginning in 1875.

His spectre was first sighted in September 1896 by comic actor Frederic Bond, who was alone on stage that night preparing for the following day's performance. Bond slowly became aware of a presence standing behind him. When he spun around, Bond was shocked to see a ghost standing directly in front of him, dressed in the traditional costume worn by the title character in *Hamlet*. Bond then recognized the apparition as his lost friend, McCullough. Bond shouted the phantom's name in a mix of welcome and horror. No sooner had the name crossed his lips than McCullough instantly vanished.

McCullough's always-silent ghost has shown up innumerable times since, usually as an indistinct, shadowy figure. There's never a sense of intimidation when he materializes. Most people describe the spirit as "benevolent" or "friendly." The spectre is most often spotted by security guards in the middle of the night when no one else is around, but he sometimes shows up by the prompter's table during rehearsals. He'll also wander the stage and inspect the sets, nodding his head if he approves. He particularly enjoys watching the final run-through of a show on the night before it opens. His apparition has even been spied sitting in the audience!

There's another ghost story that often gets lost in the retelling of John McCullough's tale. For much of the late nineteenth century, people also encountered the phanton of a little boy in the theater. No one was ever able to identify him, and he hasn't been seen in many, many decades.

Although its actors don't normally discuss the McCullough hauntings, the National Theatre doesn't shy away from the rumors: You'll find a mention of McCullough's apparition in the "History" link on the playhouse website. If manifestations occur often enough for the theater to acknowledge them, there may be a fair-to-middling chance of spotting the spirit for yourself.

Chapter 27

The Octagon Oddities

THE OCTAGON HOUSE
1799 New York Avenue NW

What does an architect do when faced with an oddly shaped plot of land? He designs a nontraditional building to accommodate it. But the unusual look of the structure isn't the only strange thing at the Octagon House. There are ghostly goings-on as well.

The three-story brick building now called the Octagon House (or simply the Octagon) was designed by William Thornton, the first Architect of the Capitol. It was constructed between 1799 and 1801 for wealthy Virginia plantation owner Colonel John Tayloe III. Originally the house was intended as the family's winter home, but they lived there full time from 1818 to 1855.

Visitors to the Octagon are surprised that it doesn't have eight sides. It's six-sided with a "bump" in the front. Its sobriquet comes from a late eighteen and early nineteenth century custom: The word "octagon" was sometimes used to describe buildings with eight angles, not necessarily eight sides.

Tayloe and his wife, Ann Ogle, had fifteen children, thirteen of whom survived to adulthood. Tayloe's family fled the city during the Burning of Washington in 1814, but they craftily invited a friend, the French foreign minister, to stay there in their absence. The diplomat raised the French flag and sent word to General Robert Ross, who was commanding the invading British troops, that, by his occupancy of the Octagon, it was French territory. Not eager to draw the French into the war, the British respected the claim, and the Octagon was spared.

The White House didn't escape the flames, however. Fortunately, everyone was safely evacuated from the Executive Mansion, but it lay waste by the time the British left town. Tayloe allowed President Madison and his wife, Dolley, to make the Octagon their home until the White House was restored in 1817. During his residency at Octagon House, Madison signed the Treaty of Ghent, which officially ended the War of 1812.

Dolley, well known as a White House hostess, continued her extraordinary soirees during her stay at the Octagon. She would stand in front of the fireplace in the ballroom on the ground floor to greet guests. Shortly after her death in 1849, the filmy figure of Dolley's phantom began to appear standing by the mantle, and it's been seen there periodically ever since. Sometimes she's spied dancing in the room or passing through the rear door of the house heading into the garden. Her ghost is often accompanied by the scent of lilacs, which was her favorite flower and perfume. Even when she doesn't materialize, the aroma may signal her presence.

Visitors enter the Octagon through the front doorway into one of its three circular rooms. The first thing they notice is the stunning staircase that wraps around the walls from the ground level to the top floor, creating a central, oval atrium. According to legend, these steps are haunted by two of Tayloe's daughters, both of whom died in the house under similar tragic circumstances. There are differing accounts of both of their deaths, but all versions seem to agree that they were the result of disagreements between the girls and their father.

One of the daughters had fallen in love with a man that Colonel Tayloe considered an unsuitable suitor. After a vicious argument with her father at the foot of the stairs, the girl stormed up to her room, candleholder in hand. Before Tayloe could collect his thoughts, he heard a cry and a loud thud. He turned to see his daughter's broken, lifeless body on the floor in front of him. It's unknown whether she had slipped and fallen over the handrail of one of the upper landings or, distraught, committed suicide by leaping to her death.

Soon after, people began to see the shadow of a non-existent candle as it moved upward along the wall next to the staircase. Some folks have heard the girl's disembodied scream and the sickening thump as well.

One of Tayloe's other daughters was being wooed by a British officer just prior to the War of 1812. Tayloe was incensed and adamantly refused to give the girl his blessing. Undeterred, she took matters into her own hand and eloped with the young soldier. She was gone for several months, and when she finally did return to the family manse, her father treated her coldly. One evening as they silently passed on the staircase—the girl was against the rail—Tayloe's daughter slipped, tumbled down the steps, and broke her neck.

She's returned from the Beyond like her sister, but she signals her presence in an unusual way. When her lifeless corpse had hit the floor, it turned up the corner of a throw rug at the bottom of the stairs. If a carpet is placed there today, people will come into the room to discover that the same corner of the new rug has flipped itself over.

In a common variation of the tales, it was the first daughter, not the second, whose admirer was the British soldier. The argument with her father took place on the second-floor landing, from which she either fell to her death or toppled down the stairs. Besides the phantom candlelight on the wall, the girl's spectre also appears, either at the bottom of the staircase or on the second landing.

In an alternate telling of the second saga, the events take place around 1817, and the beau is not a soldier. The couple elopes, but when the daughter returns home to make amends, the encounter with her father takes place on the third-floor landing. She either falls over the rail to her death or collapses down the stairs. Her ghost now haunts the third landing and the stairs between the second and third floors.

There's no historical evidence for any of the narratives, by the way. None of Tayloe's seven daughters died in the Octagon House. But why should that stop people from telling a good ghost story?

John Tayloe died in the Octagon in 1828; his wife lived there until her death in 1855. After that, the children rented the house, first to a girls' school and then to the federal government for offices. In the 1880s it became a multi-family tenement house.

There was a legend, well-established by the late 1800s, that the servants' bells in the Octagon House often rang on their own.

American author Mary Clemmer Ames wrote about the phenomenon in her 1874 book *Ten Years in Washington*:

> It is an authenticated fact, that every night at the same hour, all the bells would ring at once. One

gentleman, dining with Colonel Tayloe, when this mysterious ringing began, being an unbeliever in mysteries, and a very powerful man, jumped up and caught the bell wires in his hand, only to be lifted bodily from the floor as the bells continued to ring. Some declare that it was discovered, after a time, that rats were the ghosts who rung the bells; others, that the cause was never discovered, and that finally the family, to secure peace, were compelled to take the bells down and hang them in different fashion. Among other remedies, had been previously tried that of exorcism, but the prayers of the priest who had been summoned availed nought.

Marian Gouverneur (wife of Samuel Laurence Gouverneur Jr., the first American consul to Foo Chow, China) wrote in her 1911 memoirs that Tayloe once asked then-commander of the Washington Arsenal General George D. Ramsay to stay in the house overnight to protect his daughters while he was away. During dinner, the servants' bells began to ring throughout the house, seemingly without end. In an attempt to silence the noise, Ramsay repeatedly yanked at the bell cord to no avail. Finally, the sounds died down by themselves.

The frequency of the bell ringing increased after Tayloe's death, to the point that his family removed the bells and cords. The sounds finally ceased, and there have been no modern reports of their return.

There's another myth associated with the servant bells, this one dating to the post-Tayloe period. Around the time of the Civil War, a cardsharp used a room on the third floor to hold his "friendly" card games. Caught cheating, he was fatally shot by one of the other players. As the scoundrel slumped and died, he clutched the nearby bell cord—which in this tale had not yet been removed. For years afterward, the ethereal sound of a ringing bell was heard in the room. A few people also saw the rogue's ghost, falling with his hand outstretched as if grasping for the bell cord. The apparition was also sometimes seen stretched out lifeless on the bed.

And that's only the beginning of the spook stories at the Octagon House.

Supposedly during the War of 1812 a British soldier murdered a slave girl (in some reports, also his secret lover) by throwing her from the third floor to the foyer. In one gruesome version of the fable, he walled up her corpse somewhere in the building. Visitors to the Octagon have heard the poor girl's distant screams but have never been able to pinpoint their source. As for the soldier, his phantom was seen by the house's caretaker, James Cypress, in the 1950s. It's possible, though, the spectre could have been the man who ran off with one of Tayloe daughters—or, perhaps, another ghost entirely.

In the 1960s, the house's doors would open and lights would turn on in the middle of the night. Over the years, other paranormal activity in the building have included footprints appearing in dust on the upper floors; the scent of food; the sounds of clashing swords, rustling silk, thumps, moans, and cries; and the hallway chandelier swinging when no breeze was present. Outside, spectral carriages and footmen have materialized.

Also, there's a spot near the foot of the stairs in which people have suddenly felt irrational, intense dread. Some folks attribute the phenomenon to the deaths of the Tayloe girls or to the spirits of Union soldiers who died in the Octagon when it was pressed into service as a hospital during the War Between the States. Perhaps, others posit, the manifestations are caused by the phantoms of runaway slaves who passed through the house when it was a stop on the Underground Railroad.

The American Institute of Architects (AIA) moved into Octagon House in 1898 and purchased it four years later. The building was named a National Landmark in 1960. The AIA still owns the Octagon, but the organization has moved its headquarters to a larger building directly behind it. In 1970, Octagon House was opened to the public as a museum. Carefully restored to reflect the time of the Tayloes and the Madisons, it offers exhibitions and special programs as well as self-guided tours and guided tours by appointment—and several ghosts.

Chapter 28

All the Pretty Horses

FORMER SITE OF THE VAN NESS MANSION
17TH STREET AND CONSTITUTION AVENUE NW

THE VAN NESS MAUSOLEUM AT
OAK HILL CEMETERY
3001 R STREET NW

*The haunted Van Ness Mansion is long gone, but it's still some-
times possible to catch sight of a group of phantom horses where
the house was located. The equine ghosts also turn up at the family mausoleum across town.*

Born in 1769, John Peter Van Ness was elected a United
States Representative from New York in 1801. He was in
Congress for just a few months before President Jefferson
appointed him to the DC militia with the rank of major. By
federal law, Van Ness had to vacate his elected office to be
in the militia, but no one pressed the issue. He continued
to serve in the House, but he decided not to seek reelection.
Van Ness stayed in the army for about two decades, rising
through the ranks until finally becoming a major general
in 1813. He fought the British during the War of 1812,
including the unsuccessful attempt to prevent the Burning
of Washington in 1814.

Van Ness was named president of the National Metropolitan Bank in 1814 and remained in that position until
his death in 1846. He was elected an alderman for the City

of Washington in 1829 and was its tenth mayor from 1830 to 1834.

In 1802, Van Ness married twenty-year-old Marcia Burns. She was from a wealthy family, socially connected, and already a noted philanthropist. After her father's death, the Van Nesses inherited a fortune.

In 1816, the couple moved into a Greek Revival–style mansion, built for them by Benjamin Henry Latrobe, second Architect of the Capitol and designer of the Decatur House. The Van Ness residence, which took three years to build, stood close to 17th Street and Constitution Avenue, in the block also bounded by 18th and C Streets. Van Ness opened his home to visitors, turning it into a popular meeting place for politicians and Washington society.

Tragedy struck when Marcia died in 1832. Devastated, Van Ness ordered a monumental mausoleum for her, which now sits in Oak Hill Cemetery. The circular, columned tomb was designed by George Hadfield and modeled after the Temple of Vesta in Rome. Because of her selfless charity work, Marcia Van Ness was the first woman in Washington to receive a funeral with public honors.

(When Mrs. Van Ness died, she wasn't initially interred at Oak Hill Cemetery. At that time, the family tomb was on the grounds of the Washington City Orphan Asylum, which was located on H Street between 9th and 10th Streets. Marcia had established the orphanage in memory of her daughter, Ann, who died in childbirth in 1822. The Van Ness tomb was moved to Oak Hill Cemetery in 1872, where it now sits on top of the highest mound at the burial grounds, serenely overlooking Rock Creek. For some reason, the original tomb on H Street has been all by forgotten and is usually left out of retellings of their story.)

Legend has it that soon after Marcia's death, her spectre returned to the Van Ness mansion. She would most often appear in an upstairs hallway, usually wearing her bonnet. Even when she didn't materialize, servants heard her disembodied footsteps throughout the building. Another haunting—girlish laughter that turned into blood-curdling screams—was attributed to the ghost of Van Ness's daughter, Ann. Needless to say, all of the sightings made it difficult for Van Ness to keep his house staff.

When Van Ness himself died in 1846, he was buried next to his wife in the family mausoleum. The funeral cortege to the cemetery was drawn by his six magnificent white horses. Before long, six spectral horses were seen galloping around the Van Ness estate at night. Some people claimed the steeds were headless!

That must have been disconcerting for the property's new owner, Thomas Green. After the Civil War, the former Van Ness mansion was leased by a variety of businesses before being purchased by the Columbia Athletic Club. Columbian College, the precursor to George Washington University, bought the property in 1903. After declining to build a campus on the site, the school sold it to the US State Department, which tore down the house in 1907 to construct the Pan American Union Building. All of that time, the phantom horses never went away! To this day people occasionally spot them on the block where the Van Ness mansion once stood.

More often, the six ethereal equines show up in Rock Creek Cemetery. On moonlit nights, they can be seen silently encircling the Van Ness mausoleum. Motorists have also encountered the snow-white stallions crossing the Rock Creek Parkway.

The idea of a half-dozen gleaming stallions haunting two city landmarks seems a bit far-fetched, but believers swear it's true. They're only two miles apart. Why not take a stroll around the Pan American Union Building then, drive out to Oak Hill Cemetery to see for yourself?

Chapter 29

The Shuffling Spectre

WOODROW WILSON HOUSE MUSEUM
2340 S Street NW

BLAIR HOUSE
1651 Pennsylvania Avenue NW

Nobody gets everything he or she wants in life, and in some cases it's an unfulfilled wish that entices a spirit to cross back from Beyond the Veil. Perhaps it's just such a yearning that's prompted the 28th president of the United States to return.

Thomas Woodrow Wilson was America's president during the First World War, the so-called "war to end all wars." Serving two terms, from 1913 to 1921, Wilson was one of the nation's few scholar-politicians—that is to say, a figure who moved from the halls of academia to the rough-and-tumble world of politics.

Wilson was born in Virginia in 1856. He earned his PhD in political science and taught at several institutions of higher learning before being named president of Princeton University in 1902. Eight years later he turned his eyes toward politics and in 1911 was elected governor of New Jersey. He had his eyes set on a bigger stage, however: He ran for president of the United States in 1912 and won.

As for his personal life, Wilson's first wife, Ellen, died in 1914. The following year he married Edith Bolling, and they remained together until Wilson's death a decade later.

Wilson's victory in his run for president had been far from certain. He wasn't his party's first choice: His fellow Democrats didn't nominate him until the 46th ballot. Wilson's Republican opponent was presidential incumbent William Howard Taft. Former president Theodore Roosevelt, upset that he failed to receive the Republican Party's nomination, formed a third party, the Progressive Party, often referred to as the Bull Moose Party. Long-shot Eugene V. Debs was also in the race, representing the Socialist Party of America. In the end, Taft and Roosevelt split the Republican vote, and the Electoral College named Wilson president, despite his having won a mere 42-percent plurality of the popular vote.

Wilson's first term was responsible for some milestone legislation that still affects the country to this day: the Federal Reserve Act, the Federal Trade Commission Act, the Federal Farm Loan Act, the Clayton Antitrust Act, the enforcement of an eight-hour work day and (following the ratification of the Sixteenth Amendment under Taft) the reintroduction of the federal income tax. Wilson was also the first president since 1801 to give a live State of the Union address before Congress.

By the end of Wilson's first term, Americans were fully aware of the worsening conflict in Europe, especially after the sinking of the passenger ship RMS *Lusitania* in 1915. Wilson struggled to keep the United States out of the war, declaring the country neutral. But German submarines were sinking ships on the Atlantic indiscriminately, directly interfering with American trade and other interests abroad. In April 1917 Wilson went before Congress and asked for a declaration of war "to make the world safe for democracy." His request was approved.

Important issues such as women's suffrage continued to cross Wilson's desk, but his second term was dominated by the events overseas. In 1918, he issued his *Fourteen Points,* in which he outlined his plans for peace after the hostilities ended. Following the armistice in 1919, Wilson traveled to Paris to help negotiate the Treaty of Versailles and to promote the creation of a League of Nations to prevent future wars.

When Wilson returned and presented the treaty to Congress, almost everyone, regardless of party, seemed to have an objection to something in the pact. Perhaps most worrisome was membership in the League of Nations. Wording in the proposed accord allowed the League to declare war and commit American troops without the prior consent of Congress. Lawmakers weren't about to give up that authority— and *could not,* according to the US Constitution. In the end, Congress never ratified the Treaty of Versailles, although it did work out separate peace pacts with all of the countries involved in the war.

Wilson embarked on a nationwide tour on September 3, 1919, to sell the League of Nations to the American people. It took a debilitating toll on his health, starting with throbbing headaches and asthma attacks. Wilson was suffering extreme exhaustion by the time he reached Pueblo, Colorado, three weeks later. In Wichita, his doctors insisted he cut the tour short, and on September 26th, the presidential train sped back to Washington.

On October 2nd, Wilson suffered a serious stroke that paralyzed the left side of his body and left him with impaired vision. (Some reports say that he went completely blind in the left eye and partially blind in the right.) Wilson was confined to bed for two months and required the use of a wheelchair for weeks after that. He used a cane for the rest of his life.

Wilson's wife and his immediate staff rallied around the president, successfully shielding him from the press for months. When he finally attended a Cabinet meeting in April 1920, he was noticeably weak and easily distracted.

Despite Wilson's limited capabilities, no one was willing to make the call that the president was unable, in the words of the Constitution, "to discharge the powers and duties" of his office. The full extent of Wilson's condition didn't become known until after his death.

Wilson managed to serve out the rest of his second term, after which he moved into a 1915 townhome on Embassy Row near Sheridan Circle. For the most part, he remained out of sight, receiving few guests. His last large public appearance was on November 11, 1923, when he made a brief Armistice Day speech on the front steps of his house. He was greeted by 20,000 well-wishers!

Wilson died of a stroke and other health-related issues in a third-floor bedroom at his home on February 3, 1924. He was sixty-seven. He was interred at the Washington National Cathedral, the only US president to be buried there. His widow, Edith, continued to reside at the house, and she died there in 1961 on December 28th—Woodrow Wilson's birthday.

Mrs. Wilson bequeathed the house and most of its contents to the National Trust for Historic Preservation so that it could be turned into a museum. The Woodrow Wilson

House opened in 1963 and was named a National Historic Landmark the following year. It was listed on the National Register of Historic Places in 1966.

Many people believe that Woodrow Wilson's spirit has returned to his former home. Folks hear his shuffling, disembodied footsteps—aided by the use of a cane—all over the house. Occasionally they'll become aware of a sound coming from the former president's bedroom: a man's voice softly crying. (Legend has it that Wilson's spectre is still distraught over his failure to convince the United States to join the League of Nations.) In the 1980s, one staff member reported the inexplicable sound of a typewriter clacking away; another heard someone playing the piano. A few people claimed they've seen the president's apparition in his rocking chair.

Woodrow Wilson's ghost has shown up at another location, also seated in a rocking chair. It's at Blair House, the official guest house of the president of the United States. Located across from the White House on Pennsylvania Avenue, the historic home was built in 1824 by Joseph Lovell, surgeon general of the United States. Francis Preston Blair, an advisor to Andrew Jackson, bought it in 1836. The residence became a popular meeting place for Jackson and his unofficial "Kitchen Cabinet." Francis's son, Montgomery, inherited the property. A consul to Abraham Lincoln, he would often host the Great Emancipator in his home.

During World War II, the federal government purchased Blair House to act as the official residence for visiting dignitaries. President Truman also lived there while the White House was being refurbished. Supposedly, Truman complained of being bothered by spirits the whole time he was there. Today, Blair House is administered by the Department of State and the General Services Administration.

Blair House isn't open to the public, but it's possible to tour the Woodrow Wilson House. A visit to the former Wilson abode might be your best chance to catch a glimpse of the twenty-eighth president—or at least his ghost.

Appendix A
The National Archives

Stories have been told about the nighttime nightmares of Washington, DC, since its earliest days as our nation's capital. In the same way political shenanigans have been fodder for the rumor mill, so too have whispers that some of the city's most colorful characters have returned from beyond the grave. The tales of terror are being told in books, magazines, on television and DVDs, and online. The following is a representative sample of some of the works used to research the Federal City phantoms.

Books

Alexander, John. *Ghosts: Washington Revisited: The Ghostlore to the Nation's Capitol.* Atglen, PA: Schiffer Publishing, 1998. Paperback, 176 pp. John Alexander "classic," revised and expanded for the Schiffer Book Collectors series.

————. *Ghosts: Washington's Most Famous Ghost Stories.* Arlington, VA: Washington Book Trading Company, 1988. Paperback, 152 pp. John Alexander's book about District of Columbia spectres is considered an essential work by any ghost enthusiast interested in the nation's capital.

Ames, Mary Clemmer. *Ten Years in Washington: Life and Scenes in the National Capital as a Woman Sees Them.* London: Forgotten Books, 2012. Paperback. 660 pp. Originally published in 1874 by Queen City Publishing Company of Cincinnati, Ohio. Relates the tale of the ghostly servant bells at the Octagon House.

Apkarian-Russell, Pamela E. *Washington's Haunted Past: Capital Ghosts of America*. Charleston, SC: The History Press, 2006. Paperback, 128 pp. Haunted sites covered in the book include the White House, the Capitol, Ford's Theatre, the Octagon House, the Slidell House, Lafayette Square, the Library of Congress, and the Lincoln Memorial. Legends surrounding the spirits of Abraham Lincoln, John Wilkes Booth, Woodrow Wilson, and others are also discussed.

Gouverneur, Marian. *As I Remember: Recollections of American Society During the Nineteenth Century*. Toronto: University of Toronto Libraries, 2011. Facsimile reprint of the original 1911 edition published by D. Appleton and Company of New York. Includes a story about the ghostly servant bells at the Octagon House.

Hauck, Dennis William. *Haunted Places: The National Directory*. NY: Penguin, 1996. Paperback, 485 pp. This large reference book lists about 2,000 haunted sites in the United States. There are thirteen pages devoted to Washington, DC.

Holzer, Hans. *White House Ghosts*. NY: Leisure Books, 1979. Paperback, 220 pp. Originally published by Doubleday in 1971 in a 232-page hardcover edition under the title *The Ghosts that Walk in Washington*. Although it's been out of print from many years, this was one of the first books to document the many ghosts rumored to be inside the Executive Mansion. The work also addresses the hauntings at the Octagon House. A paranormal researcher, Holzer began publishing the results of his spirit investigations in 1963. He Studies at the University of Vienna and Columbia University. After receiving a master's degree in comparative religion, Holzer went on to teach parapsychology at the New York Institute of Technology. Before his death in 2009, he had written more than a hundred books. Holzer is often credited with coining the term "ghost hunter."

———. *Ghosts I've Met.* NY: Barnes & Noble, 2005. Hardcover, 307 pp. Reprint edition of Holzer's 1965 Bobbs-Merrill hardcover book and Ace paperback. Includes the famed ghost hunter's investigation of the Octagon House.

Horowitz, Mitch. *Occult America: White House Séances, Ouija Circles, Masons, and the Secret Mystic History of Our Nation.* NY: Bantam, 2010. The book's title speaks for itself. There are only a few ghost stories in the book; rather, it addresses American paranormal beliefs, including those held by some who have served in the White House.

Krepp, Tim. *Capitol Hill Haunts.* Charleston, SC: The History Press, 2012. Part of the Haunted America series. Paperback, 126 pp. The book contains thirty-six short stories, including accounts of nine hauntings that take place in the Capitol Building.

———. *Ghosts of Georgetown.* Charleston, SC: The History Press, 2013. Part of the Haunted America series. Paperback, 128 pp. In this follow-up book to *Capitol Hill Haunts*, author Krepp focuses on Washington's Georgetown neighborhood, relating about thirty ghostly folk tales.

Maynard, Nettie Colburn. *Was Abraham Lincoln a Spiritualist? A Medium's Memories of President Lincoln.* 2010 Kindle edition with introduction and annotations by Linda Pendleton. 114 pages. Originally published in 1891.

Ogden, Tom. *Haunted Highways.* Guilford, CT: Globe Pequot Press, 2008. Tales are based on popular ghost legends that take place on highways, lanes, and trails. Includes the story of Abraham Lincoln's phantom funeral train and the president's apparitional appearances in the White House.

———. *Haunted Theaters.* Guilford, CT: Globe Pequot Press, 2009. Ghost stories that take place in opera houses and playhouses in the US, Canada, and London. Includes the story of John Wilkes Booth's disembodied footsteps being heard in Ford's Theatre.

———. *Haunted Cemeteries.* Guilford, CT: Globe Pequot Press, 2010. A collection of campfire-style ghost stories set in graveyards, all based on existing legends. Includes a brief mention of Abraham Lincoln's spectre appearing in the Executive Mansion.

———. *Haunted Colleges and Universities.* Guilford, CT: Globe Pequot Press, 2014. More than two hundred institutions of post-secondary education—and their ghosts—are featured in this directory-format volume. Includes ethereal sightings at Gallaudet and Georgetown Universities.

Rooney, E. Ashley and Betsy Johnson. *Washington, D.C. Ghosts, Legends, and Lore.* Atglen, PA: Schiffer Publishing, 2008. Paperback, 246 pp. Rooney relates some of the city's most popular spirit legends, including those taking place at Old Stone House, Decatur House, the Hay-Adams Hotel in Lafayette Square, the Federal Aviation Administration Building, and, of course, the White House and the Capitol Building.

Thomsen, Brian M. *Oval Office Occult: True Stories of White House Weirdness.* Kansas City, MO: Andrews McMeel Publishing, 2008. Paperback, 192 pp. This book discusses the séances held by the Lincolns at the White House, Nancy

Reagan's alleged reliance on psychics, and even claims of UFO visitations. The work concentrates less on ghost lore and more on the paranormal interests and experiences of various White House occupants.

Trout, James Samuel. *Life, Adventures and Anecdotes of Beau Hickman: Prince of American Bummers.* Nabu Press, 2011. Paperback, 78 pp. This is a facsimile reprint of the original booklet published in 1879, six years after Hickman's death.

There are three other works that deserve a brief mention. They're intended for an entirely different audience: juvenile readers, aged nine to twelve.

Ghosts of the White House by Cheryl Harness (Simon & Schuster Children's Publishing, 2002)

The Ghost, The White House, and Me by Judith St. George (Holiday House, 2007)

Who's Haunting the White House?: The President's Mansion and the Ghosts Who Live There by Jeff Belanger (Sterling Publishing, 2008)

DVDS

Haunted History: Washington DC. A&E Home Video, 2009. DVD. 50 minutes. Originally aired on the History Channel. The program tells the story of America's haunted capital by profiling its ghosts—including the phantoms of Abraham Lincoln, Abigail Adams, Ulysses S. Grant, and Stephen Decatur. Commentary is provided by author John Alexander and tour operator Natalie Zanin, among others.

Websites

There are several Internet websites that list a number of haunted places in Washington, DC. Most of the legends are described in just a few sentences, but the summaries make a good starting point for further research. Here are two of my favorite sites.

haunted-places.com

An online directory of US and international haunted sites. Haunted-places.com also lists books, TV shows, and radio programs devoted to the paranormal world. It also offers a free subscription to its newsletter, the *Haunted-Places Report*.

theshadowlands.net

The Shadowlands website was founded by Dave Juliano in 1994 and is maintained with Tina Carlson. It lists 16,000-plus haunted sites from all over the world, including many found in Washington, DC. There are short descriptions of what occurs at the spots, usually less than 100 words each. The locations are sorted by the country, state, and city. The website also discusses strange anomalies such as Big Foot, Loch Ness Monster, and UFO sightings.

Paranormal Societies

As for real-life ghost hunters, there are two active paranormal organizations located in Washington, DC, that look into claims of hauntings: Dark Water Investigations and Shenandoah Shadows. You can find their contact information, along with a list of other groups that have examined cases in the nation's capital, at paranormalsocieties.com/state_list.cfm?state=dc.

In addition, the Society for Paranormal Investigation (SPI) has an operational team that investigates reports of Washington apparitions. Check them out at paranormal ghost.com.

Appendix B

Ghost Tours

Following Pierre Charles L'Enfant's masterful plan, the city of Washington, DC, is laid out in a grid pattern with most streets running north to south or east to west. Diagonal streets (later named for the states) intersect at circles, and rectangular parks offer residents and visitors open, landscaped spaces. This elegant pattern has been so transformed by growth and reconstruction since the days of the Founding Fathers that it's sometimes difficult to visualize L'Enfant's original design.

There are plenty of standard sightseeing tours of DC available, from two-hour walks in specific neighborhood to full-day coach tours and boat trips on the Potomac. Depending upon your vacation schedule and how you cope with groups, an organized excursion may be the way to go.

A few of the tours specialize in telling ghost stories along the way!

Please note that, unless otherwise noted, all of the following tours only view the exteriors of the haunted buildings. Reservations are not required for some of the tours, but it's best to check for availability. Tours depart even in light rain.

Washington Walks

819 G Street SW
Washington, DC 20024
(202) 484-1565
washingtonwalks.com

Established by Carolyn Crouch in 1999, Washington Walks offers several different themed strolls through the district, including "Capitol Hauntings" (concentrating on the Capitol Hill area) and "The Most Haunted Houses" (which begins at the Octagon and moves to Lafayette Square). The tours, which begin at 7:30 p.m. and last approximately two hours, are available from mid- to late spring and run through October. Washington Walks sometimes has a "Ghosts of the Octagon" tour available at Halloween as well. Although not designed as a ghost tour, their Sunday morning Georgetown walk passes several haunted sites mentioned in this book. Dates, times, and fees vary.

Washington DC Ghost Tours

1520 H Street NW
Washington, DC 20005
(888) 844-3999
dcghosttours.com

Washington DC Ghost Tours was founded by Frankie and Kim Harris. Two of their walks, "Ghosts of Lafayette Park" and "Capitol Hill Haunts," are offered from March to mid-November. Each tour begins at 8 p.m., lasts approximately ninety minutes, and requires less than a mile of walking. Extra tour times are added in October.

Scary DC
(202) 780-7169
scarydc.com
Founded by historian, professor, and ghost folklorist Dr. Philip Ernest Schoenberg, Scary DC conducts ninety-minute walks on weekend nights throughout the year. Dates, times, and lengths vary for its three excursions: the "Capitol Hill Tour," "Lafayette Scare," and "The Haunted Pub Tour." Scary DC has a disclaimer on its website that it "cannot be held responsible for any haunting, supernatural event, soul-possession or poltergeist activity endured before, during or after participation on the tour."

Ghost Story Tour of Washington
Historic Strolls
(301) 356-5503
historicstrolls.com
The Ghost Story Tour of Washington is presented by Historic Strolls and celebrated its fifteenth year of operation in October 2015. The walk concentrates on Lafayette Square. Participants meet at 16th and H Street next to St. John's Church for the 7:30 p.m. tour. The ninety-minute stroll, recommended for those aged eight and up, is only available on weekends in October, plus Halloween if it occurs midweek, but private tours can be arranged year-round. The tour's script was researched and written by Natalie Zanin, who was working for the Historical Society of Washington when she organized her first walk in 1998. Guides are always dressed as the ghosts of historic figures out of the city's past. Throughout the tour, guests encounter other actors in the guise of famous DC phantoms as well.

National Building Museum Ghost Tour
401 F Street NW
Washington, DC 20001
(202) 272-2448
nbm.org/programs-lectures/tours/ghost-tours.html
Exhibits at the National Building Museum tell the story of architecture, engineering, and design. The place is purported to be haunted, and a costumed guide conducts ghost tours of the museum by lantern during the Halloween season. The institution's website says the special nighttime visits combine "history, humor, and several hair-raising tales." The hour-long tours are recommended for ages ten and up. The number of tours is very limited, as is the size of each group.

DC by Foot
Free Tours by Foot
1740 18th Street NW
Suite 304
Washington, DC 20009
(202) 370-1830
freetoursbyfoot.com/washington-dc-tours
DC by Foot offers fourteen different tours of Washington. Their "Ghosts of Georgetown Walking Tour" is family-friendly, but it does involve a mile and a half of walking and takes ninety minutes. It meets outside of the Old Stone House and ends at the "Exorcist steps."

Terror Tours LLC
(844) 678-8687 (8-GHOST-TOUR)
nightlyspirits.com
Take a ghost tour, cross it with a pub crawl, and what do you get? The haunted DC pub tours conducted by Nightly

Spirits. Their first and still most popular tour, started in 2002, is the "White House Pub Tour." Accompanied by a costumed guide, the walk takes two and a half hours and stops three or four places along the way for liquid refreshment. All tours depart at 8:30 p.m. from the Occidental Grill and participants must be aged twenty-one or older. Nightly Spirits offers a similar two-and-a-half-hour tour called "Frights and Pints Old Town" across the Potomac in Alexandria, Virginia.

Yes, that's right: Alexandria. Even though this book limits itself to present-day Washington, the Old Town portion of Alexandria (along with all of what is today Arlington County, Virginia) was part of Washington, DC, from the district's inception until 1846. And it's just as haunted! Here's the contact information for two tour companies that specialize in Alexandria's spooky past.

Alexandria Colonial Tours
(703) 519-1749

alexcolonialtours.com

Alexandria Colonial Tours conducts the "Ghost & Graveyard Tour" previously offered by Doors of Old Virginia. A guide dressed in eighteenth-century costume leads the walk through Old Town by lantern light. Tours operate March through November with varying schedules and depart from the Ramsay House Visitors Center. All ages are welcome, but the tour is most appropriate for those nine and older. Working in tandem with DC Metro Food Tours, Alexandria Colonial Tours occasionally offers a second outing: "The Haunted Dine Around of Old Town." Also escorted by a lantern-carrying, costumed guide, participants on the three-and-a-half-hour culinary tour hear eerie tales of Alexandria's past while sampling three Old Town restaurants.

Footsteps to the Past

(703) 683-3451

footstepstothepast.com

Footsteps to the Past offers two different ghost walks in Alexandria's Old Town between April and November: "Historic Haunts" and "Uptown Ghost Tour." Times and dates vary. Wintertime tours are sometimes available upon special request.

DC Directory

For do-it-yourself ghost hunters, Washington, DC, is easily navigated by foot, car, or public transportation, but the sites are spread out all over the city. In the next few pages you'll find the addresses, phone numbers, websites, and other contact information you'll need to help map out your quest.

Keep in mind that many of the sites discussed in *Haunted Washington, DC* are private property, and permission must be granted to visit them. The exteriors of buildings can always be viewed from public streets, however. Remember that businesses such as restaurants, shops, and hotels prefer customers to sightseers. Be discreet if you're going into a building simply to view its interior. Entertainment venues such as theaters and museums may require a paid admission. Churches and cemeteries are consecrated ground and should be treated accordingly.

Washington, DC, is a popular tourist destination. During the summer months, crowds can be particularly heavy. Also, because of the need for increased security, getting into many of the federal sites has become difficult—at the very least, time-consuming. Plan your visit carefully and well in advance to avoid disappointment.

Chapter 1: Executive Mansion Mysteries
The White House
1600 Pennsylvania Avenue NW

Washington, DC 20500

whitehouse.gov

(202) 456-1111

Requests to tour the White House must be made through one's member of Congress no less than twenty-one days and no more than six months in advance. Foreign visitors must apply through their embassy in Washington. The self-guided tours are available Tuesday through Thursday, 7:30 a.m. to 11:30 a.m.; Friday and Saturday, 7:30 a.m. to 1:30 p.m. Hours are subject to change. Tours are free and are scheduled on a first-come, first-served basis. For more information, contact whitehouse.gov/participate/tours-and-events.

Chapter 2: The Lawmakers
The Capitol Building
1st and East Capitol Streets SE

Washington, DC 20004

(202) 226-8000 (Visitor Center)

visitthecapitol.gov

Advance reservations are required to visit areas of the Capitol beyond the Visitor Center. Tours can be arranged through the center. Once inside the Capitol, guests see the Crypt, the Rotunda, and the National Statuary Hall. US residents can also book tours through the offices of their representatives or senators; those tours often visit the legislative chambers as well.

Chapter 3: Gone, but Not Forgotten
Former Site of the Old Brick Capitol
1 1st Street NE

Washington, DC 20543

Although it's not haunted, if you're on Capitol Hill, you may want to visit the US Supreme Court building. It stands at the intersection of 1st and A Streets on the site of the Old Brick Capitol. Enter the building through the plaza doors on either side of the main staircase, Monday to Friday (except federal holidays) from 9 a.m. to 4:30 p.m. It's possible to visit portions of the building's first and ground floors, but guided tours are not provided. When court is in session, the public is admitted to oral arguments in the courtroom on a first-come, first-served basis. More information is available at (202) 479-3000; supremecourt.gov.

Chapter 4: Bookworm Bogeys
The Library of Congress
10 1st Street SE

Washington, DC 20540

(202) 707-5000

loc.gov

The Library of Congress occupies three buildings on Capitol Hill: the Thomas Jefferson Building (10 1st Street SE, between Independence Avenue and East Capitol Street), the James Madison Memorial Building (101 Independence Avenue SE), and the John Adams Building (2nd Street SE between Independence Avenue and East Capitol Street). Visiting hours vary. Admission is free. The Thomas Jefferson Building offers multiple one-hour walking tours, Monday through Friday. Note that the address given under the chapter heading is for the Jefferson building. USPS Mail should be sent to the Madison building's address on Independence Avenue.

Folger Shakespeare Library
201 East Capitol Street SE
Washington, DC 20003
(202) 544-4600
folger.edu
The library contains exhibitions, the Reading Room, and the box office for theater performances. Hours vary. Please check the library website for details.

Chapter 5: *Semper Fi*
Marine Barracks
8th and I Streets SE
Washington, DC 20003
(202) 433-4073
barracks.marines.mil
The post is not open to tourists or casual visitors.

Commandant House
801 G Street SE
Washington, DC 20003

Old Howard House
9th Street between G and I Streets SE
Washington, DC 20003
The anonymous frame house, one of several homes bordering the Marine Barracks, is a private residence and doesn't welcome visitors.

Chapter 6: The Commandant
Washington Navy Yard
8th and M Streets SE
Washington, DC 20003
Tingey House is located on the grounds of the Navy Yard. Visitors need permission to enter the base. The home itself, also known as Quarters A, is a private residence.

Chapter 7: Dead End
Congressional Cemetery
1801 E Street SE
Washington, DC 20003
(202) 543-0539
congressionalcemetery.org
The historic cemetery is still an active graveyard, and the grounds are open to visitors from dusk to dawn. Congressional Cemetery offers easy-to-follow maps and background information for sixteen different self-guided tours, with themes ranging from the "Burning of Washington" to "Women of Arts and Letters." Copies are available at the gatehouse or for download online. There are free, docent-led tours departing from the main gate at 11 a.m. every Saturday from April through October. There's also an escorted Civil War tour beginning at 1 p.m. on the third Saturday of each month.

Eisenhower Executive Office Building
1650 Pennsylvania Avenue NW
Washington, DC 20502
(202) 395-5898
Formerly known as the Old Executive Office Building. The structure was built between 1871 and 1888 as the State, War, and Navy Building to house their departmental offices.

Today it's mostly used as office space for the White House staff. Tours are not currently available.

Chapter 8: Hello, Dolley!
Cutts-Madison House
(Also known as the Dolley Madison House)
1520 H Street NW
Washington, DC 20005
Located at the northeast corner of Lafayette Square at the intersection of H Street and Madison Place. Tours are not offered to the public.

Chapter 9: Ready, Aim, Phantom
Decatur House
1610 H Street NW
Washington, DC 20006
(202) 842-0917
whitehousehistory.org
The Decatur House is located at the northwest corner of Lafayette Square at the intersection of H Street and Jackson Place. Its front door opens onto the square, so the building has the alternate address of 748 Jackson Place. The Decatur House is currently home to the National Center for White House History, owned by the National Trust, and is operated by the White House Historical Association. Decatur House offers free, one-hour tours every Monday, excluding holidays, at 11 a.m., 12:30 p.m., and 2 p.m. Additional tours are available during the summer months and by special arrangement. The facilities can also be rented for private occasions. For tour information, check whitehousehistory .org/events/tour-the-historic-decatur-house.

Chapter 10: The Woebegone Wife
Hay-Adams Hotel
800 16th Street NW
Washington, DC 20006
(202) 638-6600
hayadams.com
The lobby and restaurants are accessible to the public, but the five-star hotel does not encourage casual sightseers.

Rock Creek Cemetery
201 Allison Street NW
Washington, DC 20011
(202) 726-2080
The grave of Marian and Henry Adams can be found in Section E. The burial site is marked by the Augustus Saint-Gaudens sculpture entitled *The Mystery of the Hereafter and The Peace of God that Passeth Understanding*, but the figure is commonly referred to as *Grief*.

Chapter 11: O Say, Can You See
Site of the Philip Barton Key Shooting
Lafayette Square
Washington, DC 20005
Key's apparition appears near the spot where he was fatally wounded in Lafayette Square on the Madison Place side of the park. The spectre has also been seen walking close to his former residence on 15th Street NW, one block east of Lafayette Square.

Chapter 12: The Tolling of the Bell
St. John's Church
1525 H Street NW
Washington, DC 20005
(202) 347-8766
stjohns-dc.org
Also seen as St. John's Episcopal Church. Tours are offered following the 11 a.m. service on Sundays, 10 a.m. during the summer months. Special tours can be arranged upon request. Otherwise, visiting hours are Monday and Wednesday through Saturday, 9 a.m. to 3 p.m.; Tuesday, 11 a.m. to 3 p.m. There are services on Sunday at 7:45 a.m., 10:30 a.m., and 1 p.m., as well as on weekdays at 12:10 p.m. St. John's is an active house of worship, so guests should visit with due respect.

Chapter 13: The Halcyon Hauntings
Halcyon House
3400 Prospect Street NW
Washington, DC 20007
(202) 298-6007
halcyonhouse.org
Halcyon House is now one of two headquarters for the S&R Foundation. Led by Dr. Sachiko Kuno and Dr. Ryuki Ueno, the organization supplies residency and fellowship programs for individuals breaking new ground in the arts, sciences, and social entrepreneurship.

Chapter 14: Cheaper by the Dozen
Old Stone House Museum
3051 M Street NW

Washington, DC 20007

(202) 895-6070

nps.gov/olst

The Old Stone House is administered by the National Park Service. It's open daily from 11 a.m. to 6 p.m., except Thanksgiving, Christmas, and New Year's Day. The garden can be visited during daylight hours and is accessible through the gate on M Street. Admission to both the house and garden is free.

Chapter 15: Good Housekeeping
Foxall House
3123 Dumbarton Street NW

Washington, DC 20007

The early nineteenth-century home is a private residence and cannot be visited. The hauntings no longer seem to be active.

Chapter 16: The Bridge Street Crossing
M Street Bridge
M Street NW

Washington, DC 20007

The M Street Bridge is found in Rock Creek Park, located at the eastern edge of Georgetown. The grounds are administered by the US National Park Service. More information about the bridge and visiting the park can be found at nps.gov/rocr/index.htm.

K Street Bridge
K Street NW
Washington, DC 20007
The K Street Bridge is actually a complex of bridges over Rock Creek and the Rock Creek and Potomac Parkway. The ghost is seen on and near the Georgetown side of the span.

Chapter 17: The Echoes of War
Georgetown Bluffs on the Potomac River
14th Street Bridge Riverbank
Washington, DC 20007
The sounds and sights of General Braddock's troops are heard at several places along the high ridge overlooking the Potomac in Georgetown as well as on the riverbank near the 14th Street Bridge.

Chapter 18: The Maidens' Curse
Three Sisters Rocks
Potomac River Just North of Key Bridge
Washington, DC 20007
Walking on the islets is not prohibited, but there's no bridge access to them from the shore. Note that river currents are unpredictable for boating. Under no circumstances should an attempt be made to swim to the rocks.

Chapter 19: The Devil's Downfall
The Exorcist Steps
Prospect and 36th Streets NW to M Street NW
Washington, DC 20007
The steep staircase has no gate and is accessible to the public, twenty-four hours a day. On October 30, 2015, a plaque

was placed at the head of the staircase, commemorating it as an official city landmark. Both director of *The Exorcist* film, William Friedkin, and the author of the novel and screenplay, William Peter Blatty, were in attendance. The famous "Take Me" scene from the movie in which Father Karras plummets down the steps can be found online at https://youtube.com/watch?v=LNihprEFxOg.

Prospect House
(Also known as Lingan-Templeman House)
3508 Prospect Street NW
Washington, DC 20007
The mansion is a private residence and cannot be visited.

Georgetown University
3700 O Street NW
Washington, DC 20057
(202) 687-0100
georgetown.edu

Gallaudet University
800 Florida Avenue NE
Washington, DC 20002
(202) 651-5000
gallaudet.edu

Chapter 20: The Lincoln Legacies
Ford's Theatre
511 10th Street NW
Washington, DC 20004
(202) 426-6924 (Superintendent, Ford's Theatre National Historic Site)
(202) 347-4833 (Box Office)
nps.gov/foth (National Park Service Webpage)
fordstheatre.org (Ford's Theatre Website)
Maintained by the National Park Service as a museum. Open seven days a week, 9 a.m. to 5 p.m. Ford's Theatre is an active playhouse, and tickets are available for many of its performances throughout the year. There are a variety of self-guided and guided tours available. Most of them include a visit to the museum, the theater auditorium, and the Petersen House. Tours of Ford's Theatre do not enter the Presidential Box or the backstage areas where Booth's footsteps have been heard. The auditorium of the theater is closed to tours when there are matinee performances. Advance reservations are strongly recommended, especially during the busy summer months.

Petersen House
516 10th Street, NW
Washington, DC 20004
(202) 426-6924
nps.gov/foth
The second floor of Petersen House has been refurnished with pieces from the Civil War period, though few are original to the house.

Mary Surratt's Former Boarding House
604 H Street NW
Washington, DC 20001
As of this writing, the former boarding house is a Chinese restaurant. Its dining room is located on the ground floor, and there's a private karaoke room upstairs. The interior of the building has been much modified over the years, but its exterior is fairly extant. The house can probably best be appreciated from the opposite side of the street.

Fort Lesley J. McNair
4th and P Streets SW
Washington, DC 20319
Visitors not affiliated with the Department of Defense must use the 2nd Street SW gate. Access is not available to the general public.

1st Street NE
Capitol Hill
Washington, DC
The spectre of Judge Joseph Holt is seen walking along 1st Street NE on Capitol Hill, heading in the direction of A Street NE, where the Old Capitol Prison stood.

Chapter 21: Do Not Disturb
Site of the Colonel Beau Hickman Hauntings
6th Street and Pennsylvania Avenue NW
Washington, DC 20004
The hotel was razed in 1892. Hickman's ghost still appears at the street corner where it stood.

Chapter 22: Dead Letter Office
The Old Post Office Pavilion
1100 Pennsylvania Avenue NW
Washington, DC 20004
(202) 485-9880
nps.gov/opot/index.htm
The Old Post Office Tower is a unit of the National Mall and Memorial Parks, falling under the jurisdiction of the National Parks Service. In October 1986, Congress renamed the Old Post Office the Nancy Hanks Center to honor the woman who had spearheaded its conservation. The bell tower, its observation deck, and the pavilion have been closed since 2014 but are scheduled to open in spring 2016 as this book goes to press. The pavilion is being converted into a hotel by the Trump Organization, but the tower will remain open to the public.

Chapter 23: Abandon All Hope
Embassy of the Republic of Indonesia
(Former McLean Mansion)
2020 Massachusetts Avenue NW
Washington, DC 20036
(202) 775-5200
embassyofindonesia.org
The building doesn't offer tours. The Consular Office, which issues visas, is open Monday through Thursday, 9 a.m. to 1 p.m.; Friday, 9 a.m. to noon. The office is closed on US federal holidays and public holidays in Indonesia.

Smithsonian Institution Building
(Also known as the Castle)
1000 Jefferson Drive SW
Washington, DC 20560
The Smithsonian Institution Building is open to visitors every day of the year except Christmas, from 10 a.m. to 5:30 p.m. Extended summer hours are determined annually.

Independence Avenue
Between 7th and 9th Streets SW
Washington, DC 20003

Chapter 24: The Ghost Suites
Willard InterContinental Hotel
1401 Pennsylvania Avenue NW
Washington, DC 20004
(202) 628-9100
intercontinental.com/Washington

Mayflower Hotel
1127 Connecticut Avenue NW
Washington, DC 20036
(202) 347-3000
marriott.com/hotels/travel/wasak-the-mayflower-hotel
-autograph-collection

Omni Shoreham Hotel
2500 Calvert Street NW
Washington, DC 20008
(202) 234-0700
omnihotels.com/hotels/washington-dc-shoreham

Chapter 25: Meigs Old Red Barn
National Building Museum
401 F Street NW
Washington, DC 20001
(202) 272-2448
nbm.org
The museum is open Monday through Saturday, 10 a.m. to 5 p.m.; Sunday, 11 a.m. to 5 p.m. Closed Thanksgiving, Christmas, and for occasional special events. There is an admission fee. Several different themed guided tours are offered, including ghost tours during the Halloween season.

Chapter 26: Final Curtain
National Theatre
1321 Pennsylvania Avenue NW
Washington, DC 20004
(202) 628-6161
thenationaldc.org

Chapter 27: The Octagon Oddities
The Octagon House
1799 New York Avenue NW
Washington, DC 20006
(202) 626-7439
architectsfoundation.org/preservation
Located at the corner of New York Avenue and 18th Street, the Octagon House is open to the public Thursday through Saturday, 1 p.m. to 4 p.m. Tours are self-guided; admission is free. Private guided tours for groups of five or more are available outside of regular museum hours upon request. There is a fee, and they last approximately forty-five minutes. For scheduling, contact octagonmuseum@aia.org.

Chapter 28: All the Pretty Horses
Former Site of the Van Ness Mansion
17th Street and Constitution Avenue NW
Washington, DC 20002

The Van Ness Mausoleum at Oak Hill Cemetery
3001 R Street NW
Washington, DC 20007
(202) 337-2835
oakhillcemeterydc.org
Oak Hill Cemetery is open weekdays, 9 a.m. to 4:30 p.m.; Saturday, 11 a.m. to 4 p.m.; Sunday and holidays, 1 p.m. to 4 p.m. Closed on Thanksgiving, Christmas, and New Year's Day. Access to the burial grounds is restricted during funerals and inclement weather. A map marking the site of the Van Ness mausoleum can be downloaded from the cemetery's website.

Chapter 29: The Shuffling Spectre
Woodrow Wilson House Museum
2340 S Street NW
Washington, DC 20008
(202) 387-4062
woodrowwilsonhouse.org
The Woodrow Wilson House Museum is open Tuesday through Sunday, 10 a.m. to 4 p.m.; closed Monday, major holidays, and occasionally during inclement weather. There is limited access to the second and third floors for those with mobility issues. There is an admission fee.

Blair House
1651 Pennsylvania Avenue NW
Washington, DC 20503
blairhouse.org
Tours are not available.

ABOUT THE AUTHOR

Tom Ogden is one of America's leading experts on the paranormal and, as a professional magician for the past forty years, he has a special insight into ghost phenomena, hauntings, and all things that go bump in the night.

Ogden's first book, *200 Years of the American Circus*, was released in 1994. The American Library Association and the New York Public Library named it a "Best Reference Work," and Tom was subsequently profiled in *Writer's Market*. Ogden's other early books include *Wizards and Sorcerers* and two magic instructional books for the Complete Idiot's Guide series.

In 1998, Tom Ogden released *The Complete Idiot's Guide to Ghosts and Hauntings*, now in its second edition. *Haunted Washington, DC* is his tenth book of ghost stories for Globe Pequot.

Known as "The Ghost Guy," Ogden has been interviewed by numerous radio programs, podcasts, and periodicals, and he's in demand as a speaker on the Spirit World. His original ghost videos can be found on his "Hauntings Channel" on YouTube, and he is a member of the Paranormal Investigation Committee of the Society of American Magicians.

Tom Ogden resides in haunted Hollywood, California.